T0328659

Cambridge Elements ≡

Elements in Child Development
edited by
Marc H. Bornstein
National Institute of Child Health and Human Development, Bethesda Institute
for Fiscal Studies, London
UNICEF, New York City

THE ADOPTED CHILD

David Brodzinsky
Rutgers University

Jesús Palacios
University of Seville

CAMBRIDGE
UNIVERSITY PRESS

Shaftesbury Road, Cambridge CB2 8EA, United Kingdom

One Liberty Plaza, 20th Floor, New York, NY 10006, USA

477 Williamstown Road, Port Melbourne, VIC 3207, Australia

314–321, 3rd Floor, Plot 3, Splendor Forum, Jasola District Centre, New Delhi – 110025, India

103 Penang Road, #05–06/07, Visioncrest Commercial, Singapore 238467

Cambridge University Press is part of Cambridge University Press & Assessment, a department of the University of Cambridge.

We share the University's mission to contribute to society through the pursuit of education, learning and research at the highest international levels of excellence.

www.cambridge.org
Information on this title: www.cambridge.org/9781009454445

DOI: 10.1017/9781009339193

© David Brodzinsky and Jesús Palacios 2023

This publication is in copyright. Subject to statutory exception and to the provisions of relevant collective licensing agreements,no reproduction of any part may take place without the written permission of Cambridge University Press & Assessment.

First published 2023

A catalogue record for this publication is available from the British Library

ISBN 978-1-009-45444-5 Hardback
ISBN 978-1-009-33918-6 Paperback
ISSN 2632-9948 (online)
ISSN 2632-993X (print)

Cambridge University Press & Assessment has no responsibility for the persistence or accuracy of URLs for external or third-party internet websites referred to in this publication and does not guarantee that any content on such websites is, or will remain, accurate or appropriate.

The Adopted Child

Elements in Child Development

DOI: 10.1017/9781009339193
First published online: December 2023

David Brodzinsky
Rutgers University

Jesús Palacios
University of Seville

Author for correspondence: David Brodzinsky, dbrodzinsk@comcast.net

Abstract: This Element overviews recent research on children's adjustment to adoption and its relevance for key questions addressed in developmental science. First, a historical perspective on trends in adoption practice and adoptive family life is offered. Second, research on children's adjustment to adoption is reviewed, including the impact of early adversity on their development, as well as biological and social factors related to their recovery from adversity. Third, factors impacting adoptive identity development are examined, followed by research on open adoption and adoption by sexual minority adults. Fourth, different types of postadoption support and services that facilitate family stability and children's emotional well-being are analyzed. Finally, conclusions are drawn, and recommendations for future research and practice are offered.

Keywords: adoption, adoption adjustment, recovery from early adversity, adoptive identity, postadoption support and services

© David Brodzinsky and Jesús Palacios 2023

ISBNs: 9781009454445 (HB), 9781009339186 (PB), 9781009339193 (OC)
ISSNs: 2632-9948 (online), 2632-993X (print)

Contents

1 Introduction

The study of adopted children and their families has a long and rich history, dating back almost a century. Research and scholarly articles on adoption have been authored by professionals in numerous countries and multiple disciplines, including psychology, psychiatry, behavior genetics, social work, sociology, neuroscience, anthropology, history, law, and education. This area of study has contributed to a better understanding of some of the most important questions addressed by developmental and family researchers and scholars such as: (a) To what extent is development influenced by genetics versus environment? (b) What is the impact of early adversity and trauma on children's developmental trajectories? (c) To what extent and under what conditions are children able to recover from early adversity, and is there a critical period after which previously experienced adversity has an enduring consequence? (d) Is there an ideal family form in support of children's well-being, and are children disadvantaged when they are reared outside of their biological family? (e) How are children's self-esteem and identity affected when they grow up outside of their family of origin, as well as outside of their racial, ethnic and cultural heritage? (f) What ecological factors shape children's development and adjustment? (g) When individual and family adjustment go awry, what type of services and supports facilitate emotional healing and healthier family relationships? In keeping with the spirit of the series, *Elements of Child Development*, we explore these questions in the context of research and writings on adopted children and their families. Before doing so, however, it is necessary to review some important trends in adoption practice and adoptive family life to highlight the tremendous diversity that characterizes the makeup of adoptive families and the lived experiences of adopted individuals. We also highlight different theoretical approaches to the study of adopted children and their families.

1.1 Historical and Contemporary Trends in Adoption

Adoption involves the legal transfer of parental rights and responsibilities from biological parents to adoptive parents. Depending on the country in which a family resides, adoption is governed by national, regional, or state law. Although there is considerable diversity in how adoption is practiced from country to country, the legal basis of adoption can be traced to the earliest civilizations. Adoption is referenced in the Bible and in the codes and laws of such ancient societies as the Babylonians, Egyptians, Hebrews, Hindus, and Chinese. Unlike today, most adoptions in ancient societies involved the adoption of adults, typically males, and was a vehicle to ensure inheritance rights and the continuity of the family, to meet the requirements to hold public office, for religious purposes, or to forge an alliance between separate, but potentially rival, groups (French, 2019).

In most countries, the shift in adoption practice toward focusing on the interests of vulnerable children did not emerge until the mid-nineteenth to early twentieth centuries. In the United States, for example, the first adoption statutes were passed by the state of Massachusetts in 1851. For the first time, there was an explicit recognition in law that adoption was to promote the welfare of children needing placement outside of their biological family. Although other states soon passed similar legislation, it was not until 1929 or thereafter that other states and different countries instituted some form of judicial oversight regarding adoption. Initially, adoption involved children born in the same country as the adopters (domestic adoption). However, for reasons to be discussed below, intercountry adoptions, and in some countries, foster care adoptions, emerged as alternatives for those wishing to adopt. Together with other changes that will also be examined, such as the emergence of open adoption or adoption by gay and lesbian adults, adoption has become a complex phenomenon that affords new opportunities and concerns for children and adults as well as for those interested in the study of this form of family life, parenthood, and identity.

1.2 Characteristics of Adopted Children, Adoptive Parents, and Adoptive Families

What type of children are most often adopted and who are viewed as suitable to be adoptive parents? The answers to these questions are complex, have changed over time, and vary from one country to another. As the birth rate declined following World War I and the influenza epidemic of 1918, US public interest in adoption as a form of family building increased dramatically, a change that also occurred in other countries in connection with their own unique circumstances. Most adopting adults at the time were heterosexual infertile couples wanting to adopt newborn babies; in contrast, older children, those with special medical and mental health needs, and those who were part of a sibling group were seldom considered for adoption. Over time, the desire for adoptable babies soon exceeded the number available for adoption. This trend reflected the growing availability of contraception and abortion, which reduced the number of babies being born, as well as less social stigma associated with out-of-wedlock pregnancy and single parenthood, and increasing availability of social programs supporting the ability of parents to keep their children.

As a result of the decline in adoptable babies, some US adults began to look outside the United States as a means of building their family. For example, following World War II and especially the Korean and Vietnam Wars, large numbers of orphaned children were adopted by US citizens. Although in some places, such as the United Kingdom, domestic adoption was always preferred, many other Western countries also pursued intercountry adoption, with the number of international placements increasing rapidly from the late 1980s to 2004, when international placements peaked in most Western countries before a sharp decline. For example, in the United States, approximately 23,000 intercountry adoptions occurred in 2004, whereas by 2021 the number had dramatically declined to 1,785. A similar phenomenon has been observed in many other countries (e.g., during the same period, intercountry adoptions in a smaller country like Spain changed from 5,500 to 170). The reasons for the decline in intercountry adoptions are complex and involve, among other factors, legal and ethical concerns regarding how intercountry adoptions were being practiced in both "sending countries" (i.e., the child's country of origin) and "receiving countries" (i.e., where prospective adoptive parents reside), greater support for domestic placements in sending countries, and fewer infants or young children being made available for adoption by sending countries (Palacios, Adroher, et al., 2019).

Another important change in adoption practice concerned children who lingered in foster care. In the United States, for instance, prior to the 1980s, adoption of foster children from state care was uncommon. Because many of these children were older and had a history of adversity including prenatal exposure to drugs or alcohol, neglect, abuse, exposure to domestic violence and parental mental health problems, and/or multiple foster placements, they often were considered "unadoptable" and, consequently, child welfare agencies made relatively little effort to recruit prospective adoptive families for these young-sters. In 1980, however, the US government passed legislation which sought to create family permanency in the lives of children lingering in foster care. This landmark legislation, as well as subsequent legislative acts passed over the next three decades, emphasized the importance of timely permanency planning for children who were unlikely to be returned to their birth family. As a result, large numbers of foster children were legally freed for adoption, not only providing them greater family stability, but improving their health and emotional well-being. Currently, adoption of foster children represents the single greatest source of children for US citizens wishing to build or expand their families through adoption. A similar trend can be seen in other Western countries, where permanence and stability have become guiding principles of child protection regulations and policies.

The child welfare field has also witnessed remarkable changes in those who are viewed as acceptable adoptive parents. In the past, adoption agencies employed quite restrictive criteria in determining which adoption applicants were suitable to adopt children. In most cases, adoptive parents were middle-class to upper-class, married, white, infertile, heterosexual couples, usually in their 20s to early 40s, and free of disabilities or significant health problems. In contrast, single and older adults, racial minority adults, sexual minority adults, fertile couples, those from lower- or working-class backgrounds, adults with disabilities, and foster parents were seldom approved for adoptive parenthood. This practice was based on uninformed and biased views of what type of family best serves the interests of children. However, as developmental and family research began to show that family structure was much less important for supporting healthy child development than family processes (Golombok, 2015), adoption agencies began "screening in" applicants as opposed to "screening them out." Today, child welfare practice focuses more on identifying prospective adoptive parents who have the motivation and ability to meet the needs of children waiting to be adopted, and who understand and accept the challenges that often accompany adopting children with early adverse life experiences. Applicants' marital status, age, race, income level, foster parent status, and sexual orientation are no longer barriers to adopt children in an increasing number of countries, although almost all sending countries object to placing children with sexual minorities. Moreover, even in the United States, where such adoptions are legal, adoption agencies with religious affiliations sometimes have policies of not placing children with LGBT adults (Brodzinsky, 2012). Despite these types of restrictions, there is clearly greater diversity today in most Western countries in terms of who is building or expanding their family through adoption.

The racial, ethnic, and cultural makeup of adoptive families has also changed over time. In the past, most adoptions involved in-racial or in-ethnic place-ments, usually with non-Hispanic White parents adopting White children. With the emergence of intercountry adoption and domestic foster care adoption, many adoptive families are now characterized by parents and children who do not share the same race, ethnicity, or cultural heritage.

A final change in adoption practice and in adoptive family life is the growing numbers of adoptive and birth families who have some level of contact with one another following adoption placement. For most of the twentieth century, adoptions were closed and strictly confidential, with no identifying information shared or contact between the adoptive and birth families. However, beginning in the 1970s and 1980s, some adoption professionals and adult adoptees began advocating for open adoption, resulting in adoption researchers starting to explore the impact of postadoption contact on adoptive and birth family mem-bers, including the adopted child. In contrast to the dire warning of opponents of open adoption, research indicated that in many cases contact between the families could be especially positive for adoptive parents, adopted children, and birth parents (Grotevant, 2020). As will be discussed later, contact between adoptive and birth families in domestic placements is becoming more common in a growing number of countries. Although such contact is less common in intercountry adoptions, some internationally adopted individuals are also seeking contact with birth relatives in their country of origin.

These changes in adoption policies and practices suggest that there is no such thing as a "typical adoptive family" or a "typical adopted person." Adoptive families are highly diverse in their makeup, and the lived experiences of adopted individuals are also extremely diverse and constantly changing. Therefore, in considering questions related to the adjustment of adopted persons and their families, it is important to examine a wide range of biological, ecological, interpersonal, and developmental factors impacting the lives of these individuals.

1.3 Theoretical Perspectives in Adoption Research

Although there were previous isolated studies, the earliest systematic research on adoption, unguided by formal theory, began in the late 1950s and early 1960s, with a primary focus on describing the differences in adjustment between adopted and nonadopted individuals. Later research interest focused on developmental questions such as the role of genetics and the impact of early adversity on adoptees' psychological adjustment and recovery, and the processes and factors underlying their development (Palacios & Brodzinsky, 2010). The field of specialization of researchers has guided their empirical work and the theories that could best serve to address the issues of interest. Neurobiological and psychological trauma theories have guided studies focusing on the impact of early nutritional deficiencies and other cumulative adversities on physical, neurological, and psychological development of adopted individuals, and their postadoption recovery from previous life difficulties (Johnson & Gunnar, 2011; Rutter et al., 2010; Wade et al., 2022); attachment theory has been used to understand the impact of preadoption hardships and relationship disruptions on later attachment security of adoptees and their adjustment (Dozier & Rutter, 2016); cognitive developmental theory and stress and coping theory have provided valuable insights into how children comprehend and appraise their adoption experience and cope with loss and grief (Brodzinsky, 1990, 2011b); psychodynamic theory has contributed to understanding how adoption is internalized and experienced emotionally by the adoptee (Hindle & Shulman, 2008); Erikson's psychosocial theory and narrative theories have guided insights into adoptive identity development (Grotevant & Von Korff, 2011); and lifespan developmental psychology and family life cycle theories have been helpful in examining adoption as a lifelong experience (Brodzinsky et al., 1992). In their scoping review and analysis of adoption research, Sequin-Baril and Saint-Jacques (2023) identified twenty-seven theories that have guided empirical investigators, sixteen of which originate from psychology.

For the most part, psychological theories guiding adoption research have been rather narrow in focus, examining specific aspects of the adoption experience. An exception is the application of Bronfenbrenner's bioecological model of development to the field of adoption (Palacios, 2009). The model focuses on the development of the person, embedded within a complex nesting of contextual influences, from the direct impact of immediate influences such as family, peer group, school, and health services (microsystems), to the impact of the interactions of different microsystems (mesosystems), to the indirect effects of community influences on adoption, such as governmental agencies, social services, mass media, and neighbors (exosystems); to the broader influences of culture, social values, and laws related to adoption (macrosystems). Moreover, the chronosystem adds a temporal dimension to each of the previous levels of analysis (such as age-related changes in adoption identity in connection with parents' and professionals' changing attitudes about contact between adoptive and birth families, and changing laws and policies regarding the right of adopted persons to have access to origins-related information). Bronfenbrenner's model resonates with the "specificity principle of adoption" proposed by Bornstein and Suwalsky (2021), who assert that the experience of adoption for individuals is best understood when considering its specific setting conditions, specific people, specific times, specific processes, and specific domains. Sections in this Element reflect research findings inspired by these perspectives, as well as the other ones noted in the preceding paragraphs.

Finally, efforts to integrate different theoretical perspectives can be seen in longitudinal studies that incorporate a transdisciplinary approach. For example, the English and Romanian Adoption Study (ERA) has examined genetic influences, neuropsychological functioning, cognitive development, mental health, and behavioral adjustment in children, adolescents, and young adult adoptees (e.g., Sonuga-Barke et al., 2017). Similarly, the Early Growth and Development Study (EGDS), a longitudinal investigation of adopted children, their birth parents, and their rearing parents, studied across infancy and childhood, has investigated the role of genetics, prenatal circumstances, and rearing environments on adopted children's psychological adjustment (Reiss et al., 2023). Although it focuses on the adjustment of foster children, the Bucharest Early Intervention Project (BEIP) has also been guided by several theories, including those related to neuropsychology and attachment (e.g., Wade et al., 2022). Findings from these and other longitudinal projects are reported in this Element.

2 Psychological Adjustment and Mental Health of Adopted Children

Developmental science has always been interested in the role of the environment in children's development, but researchers cannot create specific variations in rearing conditions to study the corresponding outcomes. The study of adopted children, who often experience adverse initial life conditions followed by more nurturing postadoption circumstances, provides researchers with the opportunity to study important developmental questions related to the environments to which these children are exposed, such as: Are children disadvantaged when they are reared outside of their biological family? What are the long-term consequences of early adversity for later development and to what extent can children recover after a dramatic change of rearing conditions? The comparison of adopted children to their nonadopted peers was the first strategy used in the contribution of adoption research to the study of children's development, followed by an examination of the influence of early adversity on their subsequent adjustment and their ability to recover when their life circumstances improved (Palacios & Brodzinsky, 2010). In this section and the next, the main findings from meta-analyses and recent representative studies focusing on these questions are presented.

Before describing the findings of this research, it is important to consider the reference group against which adopted children are compared. Most research compares adopted children to their nonadopted peers living in similar communities. Given that adopted children have often been exposed to preadoption adversity, whereas their nonadopted peers have not, it is common for adoptees to manifest more adjustment problems. In such cases, adoption status is considered a risk factor for children. However, when adopted children are compared to those who remain in adverse circumstances, such as living in an orphanage or institution, or with neglecting or maltreating parents, they typically manifest more positive adjustment (van IJzendoorn et al., 2019). In short, depending on the comparison group used, being adopted can be viewed as either a risk or a positive protective alternative for children in need (Palacios, Adroher, et al., 2019).

2.1 Do Adopted Children Have More Problems?

Hundreds of studies have compared the adjustment of adopted and nonadopted individuals, using different age samples, methodologies, and outcome measures. To overcome the limitations of any one study, researchers have used meta-analysis to provide a synthesis and integrated view of the research findings. One of the first meta-analyses in the adoption literature involved more than 25,000 adoptees and 80,000 nonadopted children across different studies and countries (Juffer & van IJzendoorn, 2005). Findings indicated that although most adoptees are well adjusted, they tend to have more externalizing and internalizing symptoms than nonadopted children, with adoptees overrepresented in clinical settings. However, except for use of mental health services, for which there was a large effect size, the magnitude of the group differences was modest, with overall results supporting Haaugard's (1998) thesis about the greater presence of adoptees in the more problematic range of maladjustment. This interpretation is consistent with a previous study by Sharma et al. (1996) showing that, in the midrange distribution of scores for psychological problems, there was a 1:1 ratio for adopted and nonadopted adolescents, but the ratio was more than 3:1 at the upper range of the distribution, indicating significantly more adopted youth at the extreme level of adjustment difficulties.

Behle and Pinquart (2016) published another meta-analysis based on eighty-five studies to see if adoptees were more represented in the extreme end of clinical problems. The risk of a psychiatric diagnosis was found to be approximately twice as high in adoptees as in non-adoptees, with an elevated risk for ADHD, conduct disorder, anxiety disorders, substance use, depression, personality disorder, and psychosis. The mean percentages of adoptees receiving diagnoses varied between 32 percent (conduct disorders, oppositional and defiant disorder) and 13 percent (depression). Moreover, adoptees were at 2.35 times higher risk for receiving ambulatory mental health assistance and psychiatric treatments in general, as well as 2.63 times higher risk for receiving psychiatric hospital treatment.

Another meta-analysis focused on eleven studies of internationally adopted adolescents (Askeland et al., 2017). Once again, more problems were identified in the adopted group, with higher scores for total behavior problems and externalizing difficulties, but not for internalizing problems. The difference was larger when relying on parents' reports than adoptees' self-reports, suggesting that parents could be over-estimating their children's problems or that teenagers could be under-reporting their difficulties. Also, larger differences were observed in studies using clinical categories than when symptoms were assessed on a continuum. The use of diagnostic labels would explain why register-based studies, which tend to rely on categorical data, report larger estimates of mental health problems in adoptees.

Although adoptees' propensity to manifest higher levels of adjustment difficulties could explain their overrepresentation among children receiving mental health services, there could also be a referral bias on the part of adoptive parents. Adoptive parents have a greater propensity to seek professional services even when their children's problems are not especially serious, suggesting that they may be unduly sensitive to the challenges associated with their children's difficulties (Warren, 1992). However, this bias does not seem sufficient to explain the overrepresentation of adoptees in clinical settings, especially those in inpatient facilities. For example, adopted youth are disproportionately represented in residential treatment facilities (Brodzinsky et al., 2016). Although adoptees represent only slightly more than 2 percent of the US child population, 25–30 percent of youth enrolled in these programs were adopted. Compared to their nonadopted peers in the same facilities, adopted youth manifested more attention problems, impulsivity, oppositional behavior, attachment difficulties, trauma symptoms, identity issues, fear of rejection, and problems with empathy.

When present, adoptees' adjustment difficulties appear more enduring than transient. This is illustrated in a longitudinal study of international adoptees placed beyond the age of 4 years and followed for 3 years (Helder et al., 2016). For these children, externalizing problems remained as an area of difficulty, with some worsening over time in internalizing problems as well. A similar outcome for externalizing problems was reported in the longitudinal studies by Paine et al. (2021) and Nadeem et al. (2017), in which a significant proportion of the children (20 percent or more) continued to manifest problems in the clinical or borderline-clinical range over time, particularly externalizing behaviors. In contrast, prosocial behavior was observed to improve significantly with more time in the adoptive family (Paine et al., 2021).

Research has also examined differences in adopted and nonadopted children in other relevant areas of functioning. Executive functioning (EF) encompasses a diverse set of cognitive abilities (e.g., sustained attention, working memory, and inhibitory control) that are crucial for social interactions and school learning. There is abundant research showing the negative impact of early deprivation and its enduring consequences on EF. Research comparing EF abilities in community samples of never-institutionalized children and those with institutional experience who were later placed in foster care or in adoptive families has documented the persistence of EF difficulties in the latter groups. These difficulties have been observed shortly after adoption (Hostinar et al., 2012), as well as several years later, as in the study of children adopted in Spain from Russian institutions and examined 7 years after their adoptive placement (Peñarrubia et al., 2020). The persistence of EF problems following early adversity has also been observed in studies with a longer follow-up. In the BEIP, children who remained in institutional care were compared to those who started in institutions but were later placed in high-quality foster care, as well as to a group of community-based, never-institutionalized children. Although improvements were observed in some aspects of EF, the difficulties of the foster care group in EF functioning persisted during childhood and adolescence

(Wade et al., 2019). Together with other difficulties, such as behavioral problems and linguistic deficiencies, persistent EF problems may explain a lower academic attainment in the comparisons with nonadopted classmates (Brown et al., 2017).

In contrast to the persistence of EF problems for children placed in foster care in the BEIP longitudinal study, there was significant improvement in IQ in the first years after placement, with remarkable stability in the following years (Fox et al., 2011). The impact on intelligence of a more stimulating environment was also shown in a Swedish study based on national register data, in which the IQs of more than 2,500 male siblings separated by adoption were studied at the age 18–20 years (Kendler et al., 2015). IQs of adopted-away individuals were higher than those of their full siblings reared in their biological home environment, reflecting the more stimulating context provided by adoptive parents with higher education.

Positive changes in attachment behaviors have also been observed after placement in adoptive families. For example, a longitudinal study comparing children adopted from Russia into Spanish families and a group of children in institutional care has documented significant improvements in attachment disorders for the adoptees, but not for those in group care, whose difficulties persisted or worsened over time (Román et al., 2022). In addition, research has documented improvements in quality of attachment relationships for children with early adversity once placed in adoptive homes (Helder et al., 2016; Raby & Dozier, 2019).

In summary, research on the adjustment of adopted children supports two main conclusions. First, adopted children are within the normal range of adjustment in most domains of functioning, including those children with relatively low levels of preadoption adversity (Hornfeck et al., 2019), as well as those with more significant early life challenges (Nadeem et al., 2017). This finding runs counter to the stigma often associated with adoption, suggesting that most adoptees are maladjusted. It also supports the belief that adoption is an effective societal intervention for children who cannot be reared by their biological parents, and who otherwise might continue to live in adverse circumstances (Palacios, Adroher, et al., 2019; van IJzendoorn & Juffer, 2006). The second conclusion, however, qualifies the first one. Although most adoptees are well adjusted, as a group, they do manifest significantly more problems than their nonadopted agemates, with a higher percentage of problems in the clinical or borderline range of adjustment, especially for externalizing behavior (ranging from 20 percent to 30 percent) (Paine et al., 2021). The percentage of internalizing problems for adoptees compared to non-adoptees is smaller, but still above the clinical threshold, with proportions varying for different domains of functioning (8 percent for somatic problems, 15 percent for anxiety/depression)

(Nadeem et al., 2017). Finally, although the percentage of adopted children with clinically relevant symptoms is concerning, and requires the attention of adoptive parents and professionals, it is important to keep in mind that the problems of these children are substantially less than those youngsters who remain in maltreating homes. For example, Èthier et al. (2004) found that children exposed to continued chronic maltreatment manifested behavior problems above the clinical threshold, ranging from 69 percent in their initial assessment to 75 percent 6 years later.

2.2 The Influence of Preadoption Adversities

As previously noted, many adopted children experience early adversity and trauma prior to adoption placement. Understanding the relation between these early adverse experiences and later developmental outcomes has been of considerable research interest.

Meta-analytical evidence based on intercountry adoption studies has documented that depriving preadoption experiences put adopted children at increased risk for behavioral maladjustment (e.g., Juffer & van IJzendoorn, 2005). Most of these studies, however, use age at adoption placement as a global proxy for preadoption adversity because there is usually little information about children's preadoption experiences (Rutter et al., 2010). Even when studies can add more information about preadoption adversity, such as type of care prior to adoption (e.g., institution vs foster care) as well as limited information provided by adoptive parents, the percentage of variance explained by the known preadoption adversities is small (Finet et al., 2018).

Fortunately, domestic adoption research generally has access to detailed information about the child's preadoption circumstances. This is illustrated by a Welsh prospective longitudinal study of children placed for adoption (Paine et al., 2021). Besides the child's age at placement, available information included the number of days spent with birth parents and in foster care before adoption, the number of moves prior to the adoptive placement, and ten categories of adverse childhood events (ACEs), including childhood abuse and household dysfunction. Results indicated strong correlations between different preadoption adversities (ACEs, time with birth parents, number of moves, time in care) and persistent negative impacts on adopted children's internalizing and externalizing scores over time. The number of preadoption adverse events *per se* and in interaction with number of moves while in care were significantly related to children's problems. However, after about a year and a half in caring families, the long-term effects of ACEs on externalizing problems were no longer significant, which the researchers suggest reflects the positive experience of living with loving and stimulating families for children with more preplacement adversity.

Murray et al. (2022) also had access to detailed information about children's preadoption adversities in their study of suicidal ideation and suicidal behaviors. Before being adopted, nearly all adolescents in their sample had experienced at least one type of potentially traumatic event (93.5 percent), most had experienced more than one type (73 percent), and many experienced all four types of maltreatment considered (physical abuse, sexual abuse, psychological maltreatment, or neglect) (17 percent). Compared to nonadopted peers, adolescents who were adopted had increased likelihood of endorsing both suicidal ideation and suicidal behavior, but when polytrauma and traumatic stress symptoms were added into the predictive models, adoption status was no longer a significant predictor for either indicator, while polytrauma by itself was significantly related to both. Once again, the more detailed information about preadoption adversities, frequently absent in adoption research, is essential to provide the context for a thorough understanding of adoptees' problems.

An important implication of this discussion is that, more than any single predictor, the accumulation of preadoption adversities helps to explain postadoption adjustment difficulties. This conclusion is well illustrated in the German study by Hornfeck et al. (2019) assessing multiple preadoption risk factors, including prenatal risk (e.g., maternal psychopathology and substance abuse during pregnancy), experiences of emotional, physical, and sexual abuse and neglect, and number of placement changes before adoption (with relatives, in foster or institutional care). As the number of risk factors increased, the likelihood of showing serious emotional and behavioral problems increased from 0 percent (no risk factors present) to 50 percent (four risk factors present).

2.3 The Role of Age at Adoptive Placement

Does age at adoption matter? Is there a specific adoption placement age after which children can be considered at risk for developmental difficulties? This last question is tied to a classic issue in developmental science, namely the existence of critical/sensitive periods (Bornstein, 1989): Is there a critical period for positive and negative experiences to leave a permanent imprint on a child's developmental trajectory? Is there an age threshold after which recovery is compromised? The study of children exposed to significant adversities during known periods of time and to more positive caregiving experiences afterwards sheds light on this key developmental issue. This problem is addressed before responding to the more general question about the importance of age at adoption.

For the critical/sensitive period question, two longitudinal studies following the early adversity-later enrichment paradigm are particularly relevant. One is the ERA study involving children removed from very depriving Romanian institutions between a few weeks to 42 months and placed with advantaged adoptive parents in the United Kingdom (Sonuga-Barke et al., 2017). The second study is the BEIP, in which children between 6 and 31 months were recruited from institutions in Bucharest and then randomized to either continue in institutional care or to be placed in a high-quality foster care program (Nelson et al., 2019). Both the ERA and the BEIP studies have followed their participants from early childhood to young adulthood, using comparison samples.

The ERA results are more in accordance with the classic critical period concept. Because problems such as cognitive impairment, inattention-overactivity, disinhibited attachment, and autistic-like social behaviors were consistently present in virtually all those adopted after the age of 6 months, but not before this age, the suggestion is that introducing enriched family conditions before the 6-month threshold facilitates normal development (Sonuga-Barke et al., 2017). The BEIP conclusions are more complex and nuanced (Nelson et al., 2019). The main difference in this study was between those exposed to enriched circumstances before or after 24 months. But, more importantly, both the deprivation effects and the subsequent recovery varied by domain. Some domains were apparently unaffected by exposure to adversity (e.g., face and emotion processing), other domains showed evidence of improved caregiving effects but not evidence of critical period effects (e.g., social competence, psychiatric disorders), and other domains had little improvement after placement in a family environment (e.g., some executive functions, and ADHD). The idea of a developmental critical period is also undermined by the fact that, within broad constructs such as IQ, language, and attachment, there seems to be different critical periods for different underlying processes (Nelson et al., 2019), as discussed in the next section.

In summary, the existence of one critical or sensitive period that determines when recovery after initial adversity is unlikely has little empirical support (Brodzinsky et al., 2022). Across and within domains, there are cascades of different sensitive periods under the influence of multiple experiential and biological factors. Later acquisitions can compensate for skills not well established previously, although in other cases poor initial acquisitions impair the development of more advanced skills (Nelson & Gabard-Durnam, 2020). With enriched stimulation, the possibility of functional modifications extends into adolescence, as illustrated with three examples. The stress system response is recalibrated in adolescence in the presence of significant improvements in the supportiveness of the environment (Gunnar et al., 2019). High-quality caregiving in adolescence is associated with improvements in EF and behavioral adjustment, with stronger associations during adolescence than in the preceding years (Colich et al., 2021). When adoptive mothers have a secure state of mind, the association with positive changes in the adoptees' attachment representations is more evident in adolescence than in the preceding years (Pace et al., 2019).

Does this discussion imply that age at adoption is irrelevant for understanding later adjustment? Evidence from individual studies is inconsistent, with some reporting a lack of association between age at adoption and behavioral adjustment (e.g., Finet et al., 2018), and others supporting the view that older age at placement results in detrimental outcomes for children (e.g., Helder et al., 2016). Meta-analytical evidence is also contradictory, with studies looking at behavioral adjustment indicating a lack of evidence for a decisive influence of age at placement (Juffer & van IJzendoorn, 2005), and studies looking at psychiatric disorders and treatment in mental health services reporting a significant association between older age at adoption and greater prevalence of disorders (Behle & Pinquart, 2016). In terms of the previous discussion of Haaugard's (1998) proposition of adoption-related risk, it may be that age at adoption is more critical when the extreme end of clinical problems is considered.

A good example of the importance and limitations of age at placement can be found in research on adoption instability and breakdown. An older age at adoption is related to increased risk of serious placement difficulties (Palacios, Rolock, et al., 2019). However, such difficulties are not the consequence of one isolated factor, but of an accumulation of risk factors in the child (including a longer exposure to previous adversities, with more separations, relational distrust, and insecurity, and with more emotional and behavioral dysregulation), in the adoptive parents, and in postadoption professional support (Palacios, Rolock, et al., 2019). Although age at placement is a significant predictor of adoption breakdown, most late adoptions are stable (e.g., Rushton & Dance, 2006). The conclusion is that age at adoption provides insufficient information for understanding the role of specific adversities and does not address how child, parent, or family characteristics might influence the impact of such adversity on children's development and adjustment. In subsequent sections, these influences are studied in more detail.

3 Postadoption Recovery

Having analyzed the impact of early adversity on adopted children's development, we now turn to factors influencing patterns of recovery from these difficult life circumstances. Postadoption recovery has been documented in numerous studies (e.g., Leroy et al., 2020), and meta-analyses have reported a "massive catch-up" in all aspects of growth, cognitive and socio-emotional development once children are placed in caring and nurturing adoptive families (van IJzendoorn & Juffer, 2006). The two questions addressed in this section are to what extent this recovery process varies by domain (differential plasticity) and differs between individuals (genes and resilience). A third related topic, the family environment impacting postadoption changes, deserves more detailed attention and is discussed in the following section.

3.1 Differential Plasticity

The term "plasticity" refers to the capacity of the organism to adjust to changing circumstances and demands of the environment, but "differential plasticity" indicates that such capacity is not homogeneous across different developmental domains (Palacios et al., 2014). As Nelson et al. (2019) noted, prolonged positive stimulation in a family context may overwrite the effects of early deprivation, but not in all domains. In their examination of changes in growth and in several important psychological dimensions, adoption researchers have documented these differences.

3.1.1 Physical Growth

The psychosocial growth failure caused by negative nutritional and environ-mental circumstances (Johnson & Gunnar, 2011) translates into shorter stature, lower weight and body mass index (BMI), and smaller head size (a good predictor of brain volume during infancy and childhood), with an impact on neurocognitive and other behavioral difficulties (Kroupina et al., 2015). Once adopted, children with a delayed growth profile improve in their anthropometric parameters, with a marked recovery in comparison to those remaining in negative circumstances (van IJzendoorn et al., 2007). Overall, there is a substantial catch-up, regardless of child's country of origin, gender, and age at adoption (Ivey et al., 2021). Recovery is more complete for those placed earlier or after less adversity, with an accelerated improvement particularly in the first postplacement years and for those with more severe delays at placement (Canzi et al., 2017; Palacios et al., 2011). In other cases, catch-up may not be as complete, but close to anthropometric normal ranges (Gunnar & Reid, 2019; Johnson & Gunnar, 2011).

Compared to height, weight, and BMI, improvement in head circumference is slower and less complete, although still substantial (Johnson et al., 2018; van IJzendoorn et al., 2007), reflecting the differential plasticity principle in the physical growth domain. This principle is also observed within the brain. As summarized by Brodzinsky et al. (2022), total gray matter volume and cortical thickness are affected negatively by early deprivation and seem not to change significantly after adoption, which is important given their involvement in vital functions (e.g., speech, memory, impulse control). However, the volume of white matter and the white matter track integrity show substantial recovery once early adversity ends, which is also important given their involvement in the transmission of information between different areas of the gray matter. Brodzinsky et al. (2022) concluded that, within the brain, the process of recovery may largely consist of being better able to effectively use the neural circuits that survive early adverse care.

Leaving aside for a moment the differential plasticity issue, a potential implication of accelerated growth is worth mentioning, namely, precocious onset of puberty, associated with a shorter mean final height. This outcome appears more likely to affect those who experienced rapid catch-up growth after being growth stunted before adoption (Gunnar & Reid, 2019). In addition, the EGDS showed that asynchrony in puberty-related body changes was associated with a higher risk of peer victimization for adopted girls, but a lower risk for boys (Natsuaki et al., 2021).

Another health-related issue that is receiving increasing attention in adoption research is prenatal exposure to alcohol leading to fetal alcohol syndrome (FAS) or fetal alcohol spectrum disorder (FASD). The potential effects include facial dysmorphology, growth retardation, and neurological and psychosocial problems. The incidence FASD in the general population has been estimated at 7.7 per 1,000 individuals, but it is much higher among children in the care system: 25.2 percent among children in out-of-home care in the United States and above 50 percent in adoptees from Eastern Europe (Popova et al., 2023). An adequate identification of these cases is essential to avoid both underdiagnosis and misdiagnosis as well as to help adoptive parents adequately support their child's needs (Koren & Ornoy, 2020). In addition, the use of opioids during pregnancy, often combined with other drugs such as cocaine, has been associated with abnormalities in fetal neurodevelopment, reduced brain volume and significant impairments in cognitive, psychomotor and behavioral outcomes, also increasing the risk of child removal by child welfare services (American Academy of Pediatrics Council on Foster Care, Adoption, and Kinship Care, 2018).

3.1.2 Psychological Development

For children exposed to early adversities, growth and psychological development are related, both at the time of adoptive placement (Palacios et al., 2011) and later. In the BEIP longitudinal follow-up at 42 months, for instance, each increase of 1.00 in standardized height scores was associated with a mean increase of nearly 13 points in verbal IQ (Johnson & Gunnar, 2011). Also, in the ERA longitudinal study, the relationship between institutional deprivation and both low IQ and ADHD symptoms was mediated by reductions in total brain volume (Mackes et al., 2020). In short, different aspects of development are interrelated, and the differential plasticity observed in growth can also be observed in other developmental domains.

Marked improvements in adopted children's IQ have been confirmed by meta-analyses showing significant differences, with large effect sizes, compared to those who remained in their birth families or in institutions, but no differences with current community peers (van IJzendoorn et al., 2005). The improvement was observed for adoption at different ages, as well as for different types of adoption (domestic vs intercountry). Moreover, although the IQ of those randomized to both institutional care and foster care remained negatively affected throughout childhood, the longitudinal analysis in the BEIP identified significant between-group differences at ages 8 and 12 years in the verbal comprehension subscale, with children in foster care having higher scores (Almas et al., 2016). This suggests that not all aspects of cognition present a similar profile of improvement, as noted below for changes in executive functions.

In terms of language development, meta-analytical research has shown that adopted toddlers and preschool children have language skills that are similar to those of their community peers, but during the school years their language skills fall behind (Scott et al., 2011). As the authors suggest, this conclusion appears consistent with Dalen's (2005) finding indicating that the main language difference between adopted and nonadopted children is not in daily, concrete language, but in abstract language and metalinguistic abilities so necessary for school success.

Differential plasticity also has been reported for EF in adopted children, with a significant recovery in some areas and persistent problems in others (Peñarrubia et al., 2020). Findings vary depending on methods of study, contents, and populations explored, but most studies identify impulse inhibition and attention control as the domains of greater vulnerability in children with early adversity (Wretham & Woolgar, 2017). These difficulties are at the core of ADHD and, together with the mentioned language difficulties, explain problems in academic achievement more present in those with early adversity (Anderman et al., 2022). Moreover, together with problems in emotion regulation (Perry & Donzella, 2023), EF difficulties are a transdiagnostic (i.e., cutting across different forms of psychopathology) mediator between severe neglect in childhood and psychopathology in adolescence (Wade et al., 2020).

Differential plasticity has also been observed in psychological adjustment. As reviewed previously, differences between adopted and nonadopted children and adolescents are more marked for externalized than for internalized difficulties (e.g., Askeland et al., 2017). The importance and timing of the improvement in externalized problems can be illustrated with one of the findings in the BEIP: At age 8 years, the institutional and the foster care groups did not differ in self-control, but significant differences were observed at 16 years, when the foster care group had markedly better self-control abilities, a finding attributed to a "sleeper effect," in which the benefits of positive family influences may not fully manifest until later in development (Wade et al., 2022). This finding does not imply that all improvements in externalized behavior must wait many years to be manifested, but only that positive changes linked to improved rearing circumstances exert a positive influence in the short term and later on.

Finally, differential plasticity has also been documented for postadoption changes in the attachment system including attachment disturbances, behaviors, and representations. In the longitudinal study of children adopted from Russia into Spanish families at a mean age of 3 years (Longitudinal Adoption and Institutionalization Study, University of Seville, LAIS.US), symptoms of both reactive attachment and disinhibited social engagement disorders improved during the first months in the adoptive families, with no significant differences with a comparison community group and strong differences with institutionalized children (Román et al., 2022). Also, in sharp contrast with those who remain institutionalized (Lionetti et al., 2015), positive changes in attachment behaviors have been documented in several studies, with changes observable within the first year in the adoptive family (e.g., Carlson et al., 2014) and a progression toward more secure attachments. Research showing that, in children with early adverse experiences, the development of secure attachment prevents the onset of internalizing difficulties (McLaughlin et al., 2012) underscores the importance of this achievement.

Attachment representations (a reflection of the internal working models of self and attachment figures formed on the basis of early attachment relationships) also improve after adoption, but more slowly than the other aspects of the attachment system. For example, in the LAIS.US study, in middle childhood, after 3 years in the adoptive family, all dimensions of adopted children's attachment representations were still similar to those of the comparison institutional sample (Román et al., 2012), but after 7 years in the family, a clear improvement in adopted children's representations was observed (Peñarrubia et al., 2022). Differential plasticity within the attachment representations was also observable at this follow-up, as indicators of insecurity and disorganization were still present while the other dimensions (e.g., coherence, secure base) were similar to comparison community peers. Similar changes and limitations have been described in a study with children adopted in Italy at a later age (4–8 years) and assessed in adolescence (Pace et al., 2019). As the authors indicate, the long experience in a secure family-context allowed late-adopted adolescents to improve their attachment behaviors and to create more integrated internal working models of attachment. The improvement is quite relevant not only because these representations indicate how children perceive self and others, but also due to their impact on affect regulation (particularly under stressful circumstances, when the attachment system is activated) and mentalizing (capacity to interpret behavior of self and others as motivated by feelings and thoughts, and to guide actions accordingly) (Tang et al., 2018).

When significant difficulties in psychological domains persist and children's adjustment is more problematic, the adoptive placement is at higher risk of instability or breakdown. As mentioned in the preceding section, research has consistently shown that this risk is not the consequence of an isolated factor, but the product of an accumulation of problems in the child, the parents, and the support they receive. Among the child-related factors, behavioral problems (particularly, externalized ones), attachment difficulties, and other adjustment issues (e.g., school difficulties) are often present (Palacios, Rolock, et al., 2019).

3.2 Resilience and Genes

If some developmental domains change more rapidly and more completely than others, another relevant question is whether, adopted after early adversity, some children are more susceptible to change than others. To address this issue, the concept of resilience and the analysis of genetic influences are of interest. The latter refers to a classic question in developmental science, namely, the relative influence of nature and nurture, and the debate on gene-environment (G×E) interactions. In typical circumstances, the effects of genes and environment are confounded, as both are provided by the same parents (the so-called passive G×E correlation). To disentangle their effects, behavior genetic researchers have utilized the "adoption design," whereby the genes come from the birth parents and the environment is configured by the adoptive parents. Not all the studies utilizing an adoption design are interested in adoption *per se,* so our analysis is limited to genetically informed adoption research, with the resilience paradigm as a framework.

According to Plomin et al. (2022), three stages can be identified in the history of G×E research. In the first stage, genes were not directly assessed, but the genetic risk of adopted children was estimated based on birth parents' psychopathological conditions assumed to have a genetic component. Once the tools to analyze DNA became available, a new generation of studies started, although initially the time and expense to genotype DNA variants limited the analysis to a few genes, typically those coding for neurotransmitters presumed to be related to psychopathology. However, according to Plomin et al. (2022), the heritability of complex traits and common disorders is caused by thousands of inherited DNA differences, each with miniscule effects. A new technology now allows researchers to aggregate all these genome-wide variants in a single genetic index or polygenic score, opening new ways for the third stage of genetically informed research.

3.2.1 Resilience: Adoption as a Turning Point

Resilience was defined by Masten (2011) as the capacity of a dynamic system to withstand or recover from significant challenges that threaten its stability, viability, or development. It requires the presence of both significant adversity and a positive adjustment in several developmental domains, as happens in the case of children adopted after experiences of significant adversity. Resilience is not within the person (e.g., genes) nor in the environment (e.g., rearing practices), but rather in the dynamic interplay between the two. Rutter (2006) emphasized that resilience is not a general quality that represents a trait of the individual and that genetic variants are neither a risk nor a protective factor in themselves. As Bowes and Jaffee (2013) stated, there are no "good" or "bad" genes. In the absence of environmental risk factors, genetic vulnerabilities have little or no effect on psychopathology and, conversely, in the absence of a positive environment, the expression of genetic possibilities will be limited. DNA sequences and genes are fixed, but their expression is not, and the term epigenetics refers to the reversible regulation of such expression (Bowes & Jaffee, 2013). Although previous exposure to extreme adversity may limit the possibilities of resilient adaptation to the new environment, adoption illustrates one of the "turning points" for development (Rutter, 2006) where the circumstances regulating the epigenetic process and promoting resilient functioning experience a radical change. A few examples from genetically informed adoption research attest to the results of this change.

The first illustration comes from three Swedish population studies where the genetic influence was inferred from parental psychopathology. One of the studies concerned alcohol use disorders (AUD), a condition where meta-analytical evidence has estimated heritability at 51 percent (Kendler et al., 2021). In this study, matched sibling pairs, where one child was reared by the biological parents and the other was adopted away, were compared, with AUD after age 15 years as the outcome variable. A significant reduction in the risk for

AUD was observed in adoptees compared to their nonadopted siblings, with a stronger effect in those with very high familial liability (both birth parents and at least one grandparent affected and with AUD of early onset). Another study was very similar in design and outcomes, but with criminal conviction as the variable of interest (Kendler et al., 2016). Again, results supported the strong impact of the rearing environment, with the protective role of adoption being especially significant in those at high familial risk for criminal offending (more severe and repeated crimes). The same pattern was shown for major depression, with adopted children at high genetic risk manifesting significantly reduced depression once adopted, although the protective effect disappeared if an adoptive parent had major depression or if the adoptive home experienced parental death or divorce during childhood/adolescence (Kendler et al., 2020).

Adoption as a turning point was also demonstrated by a British research team using techniques from the third generation of genetic influence studies (Cheesman et al., 2020). Polygenic scores from the UK Biobank were available for 6,311 adopted and 375,343 nonadopted individuals. The variable of interest was educational attainment, an outcome in which quantitative genetics has shown to explain approximately 10 percent of the variance. Individuals in the lowest decile of the examined genetic index attained significantly more years of education if they were adopted, a finding that the authors attribute to education-ally supportive adoptive environments and suggesting that efforts to help individuals stay in education can be more effective for those with less genetic propensity for educational success.

3.2.2 Diathesis-Stress, Differential Susceptibility, and Evocative G×E

Two models of genetic influence have been proposed, both with implications for adoption. The first model, called diathesis-stress, posits that individuals with genetic vulnerabilities (diathesis) for psychopathology present with psycho-pathological outcomes only if exposed to stressful life experiences. Findings from different adoption studies inspired by the first generation of genetically informed research support this model. In a study by Cadoret et al. (1995), a biological background of antisocial personality disorder predicted increased conduct disorder and antisocial behavior in adopted adolescents only when there was adversity in the adoptive family environment (e.g., marital problems and parental psychopathology). A similar finding was reported by a Finnish study involving a group of adopted children whose birth parents suffered from schizophrenia as well as a comparison group of adopted children without such antecedents (Tienari et al., 2004): for adoptees at high genetic risk, there was a higher incidence of schizophrenia-spectrum disorder when the adoptive family environment was conflictual and problematic, which was not true for adoptees with difficult adoptive families but without the genetic risk. In short, developmental risk is not inevitably contained in the genes, but only in the interaction between genetic risk and environmental adversities, as the resilience framework would predict.

A differential susceptibility model has also been proposed. According to Bakermans-Kranenburg and van IJzendoorn (2015), if the diathesis-stress model explores the "dark side" of the moderating role of genotypes vulnerable to negative environmental conditions, the differential susceptibility model explores the "bright side." In this model, the fundamental proposition is that some children are not only more vulnerable to adversity than others, but also more likely to benefit from enriched environments, being more developmentally plastic or malleable "for worse and for better" (Belsky & van IJzendoorn, 2017). According to this model, genotypes that in adverse contexts put children at risk for behavior problems may also make them more likely to benefit from support.

The existence of susceptibility genes has been explored using techniques from the second generation of genetic influence studies (i.e., specific gene polymorphisms that regulate the modulation of neurotransmitter systems related to different psychopathological conditions). In research on interventions aimed at improving parenting, but unrelated to adoption, meta-analytical evidence summarized by Belsky and van IJzendoorn (2017) found much stronger intervention effects in individuals with the susceptible genotypes than in the non-susceptible genotype carriers. However, the evidence from foster care and adoption studies in support of this model is mixed. A study from the BEIP showed that, in the group remaining in institutional care, children with a specific gene variant showed the highest rates of externalizing behavior ("for worse"), whereas in the foster care group, this same variant was associated with the lowest levels of externalizing behavior ("for better") (Brett et al., 2015). However, research in the EGDS, using a broad measure of child genetic liability (based on birth parent psychopathology), adoptive home variables, and measures of child externalizing problems and social competence, found little evidence of differential susceptibility (Cree et al., 2021).

Several results from the EGDS are more aligned with the evocative G×E model. This is a full adoption design that includes birth parents, children adopted within a few days of birth, and adoptive parents (Reiss et al., 2023). Associations between birth parents and their adopted children can only be attributed to genetic factors or intrauterine influences. Because this study is longitudinal, evocative effects can be examined: genetically influenced attributes in the child may "evoke" specific behaviors from the adoptive parents, which in turn will have an influence on different child outcomes. In one EDGS study (Shewark et al., 2021), birth parents' temperament was related to child negative emotionality at age 4.5 years, and this behavior evoked hostile parenting from adoptive parents at 6 years, which was subsequently related to child problem behaviors at 7 years. In contrast, adoptive mothers' warm responses at age 6 were positively associated with social competence one year later, proving once more the influence of the environment on the expression of genetic liabilities.

All previous information about resilience and the role of genetic influences presents a rich picture of the interplay between preadoption adversity and the protection brought about by adoption, a significant turning point in the life of adopted children. As the reported studies indicate, preadoption adversity refers to developmentally untoward experiences of neglect and abuse and may include some form of genetic and/or prenatal liability. Resilient functioning is a possibility when positive changes are experienced in the rearing environment. This possibility is not absolute, but dependent on the developmental domain and the level of severity of the previous adversity. For the genetic influences, no matter the G×E model considered, the potential risks for psychopathology and behavioral maladjustment will or will not be expressed depending on the characteristics of the rearing environment, the topic our attention turns to in the following section.

4 Parenting and Family Influences on Developmental Recovery and Adjustment

In the preceding section, we described technological advances that allow the aggregation of thousands of DNA variants in a polygenic score. Although the environment that influences us is also composed of a myriad of interrelated elements, the problem is that, in terms of research, we lack an "environome" similar to the genome (von Stumm & d'Aprice, 2022). Additionally, our genes and their variants do not change throughout our lives (only their epigenetic expression changes), but our environment is in constant flux.

Before examining specific parenting and family factors influencing adopted children's adjustment, three general principles of development are highlighted. First, like in all families, the impact of parenting behavior on adopted children is not unidirectional, with parents' simply influencing their children's behavior. Rather, the characteristics and behavior of children also influence the way parents react to them. In other words, the influence between parents and children is ongoing and bidirectional or transactional. As just one example, Leve et al. (2019) found that a lower inhibitory control in adopted children increased the probability of hostile interactions on the part of adoptive parents. A second general point is that parenting behavior that is effective with one child is not necessarily effective with another. For example, Kriebel and Wentzel (2011) found that adopted children with higher cumulative risk scores seemed to benefit more from child-centered parenting strategies than those with lower cumulative risk scores. Finally, a broader developmental principle also reflected in the adjustment of adopted children is that the influence of distal preadoptive factors, without disappearing, seems to diminish as children get older, while the effects of proximal postadoption experiences increase. An example can be found in the Leiden longitudinal study of international adoptees, where early malnutrition, despite having an effect on children's IQ, did not negatively affect the adopted young adult's socioeconomic success, indicating that early malnutrition may be compensated by later experiences in the adoptive family (Schoenmaker et al., 2015). Another example can be found in the aforementioned study by Paine et al. (2021) in which the influence of negative preadoption adversities on externalizing behavior ceased to be significant after more than a year in the adoptive family, a reflection of the new positive experiences for children with more preadoption adversity. As noted by Duncan et al. (2021), healthy family environments can mitigate the influence of early adversity and have an impact over and above preplacement risk factors.

Researchers have examined a variety of postadoption variables associated with children's recovery from adversity and adjustment (e.g., Duncan et al., 2021). Some are more linked to parents' characteristics, and others are related to family dynamics and socialization practices.

4.1 Adoptive Parent Factors

Various aspects of adoptive parents' mental health have been linked to children's postadoption recovery and adjustment. For example, depressive symptoms in one or both adoptive parents have been associated with their children's depressive symptoms (Liskola et al., 2018) and internalizing behavior problems (Goldberg & Smith, 2013; Hails et al., 2018). In addition, Hails et al. (2018) found that adoptive fathers' depressive symptoms moderated associations between adoptive mothers' depression and children's externalizing behavior. Postadoption depression in parents is not uncommon – with rates comparable to postpartum depression in biological parents – and is usually linked to unfulfilled and unrealistic expectations related to their children or themselves, as well as unmet support needs (Foli et al., 2012).

Parental stress is another factor linked to children's postadoption recovery and adjustment. In a sample of 7-year-old internationally adopted children placed during infancy, Gagnon-Oosterwaal et al. (2012) reported that children's preadoption adversity (assessed as health and developmental problems at placement) was positively associated with current internalizing and externalizing problems, and that these relations were mediated by adoptive mother's current level of stress. Santos-Nunes et al. (2018) also found a link between adoptive parents' stress, often related to violated expectations, and their children's adjustment difficulties. This circumstance (violated expectations) is often present in adoptions that become unstable or break down (Palacios, Rolock, et al., 2019).

Different aspects of parenting style have been explored in relation to children's adjustment. Audet and Le Mare (2011), for example, reported that authoritarian parenting was negatively associated with inattention and overactivity problems for youngsters who experienced significant preadoption deprivation. Negative power assertive parenting strategies have also been linked to placement instability (Rushton et al., 2000). High-quality structure and limit setting by adoptive parents resulted in fewer regulation problems for postinstitutionalized children (Lawler et al., 2017). In addition, parental warmth moderated the link between children's early adversities and their subsequent internalizing behavior three years after placement (Anthony et al., 2019).

Adopted children's adjustment is also impacted by parental sensitivity (i.e., understanding children's signals and providing appropriate and prompt responses to them) and parental mind-mindedness or reflective functioning (i.e., representing and holding in mind children's presumed thoughts, feelings, and desires). In a study by van der Voort et al. (2014) of adolescents internationally adopted in infancy, maternal sensitivity in infancy and middle childhood predicted less inhibited behavior in adolescence, which in turn predicted lower levels of internalizing problems. Priel et al. (2000) also reported an association between higher maternal self-reflectiveness and decreased levels of externalizing problems in adopted children.

Parent's cognitions and attitudes about adoption play a role in children's adjustment. Some adoptive parents readily acknowledge the inherent differences between adoptive and nonadoptive families, whereas others deny or minimize such differences. Lo and Grotevant (2020) found that adoptive parents characterized by an acknowledgment-of-differences perspective during middle childhood had youth who experienced stronger feelings of attachment to their parents during adolescence.

Finally, adoptive parents' internal working models of attachment have been linked to adoptees' attachment security. For example, in a sample of Italian families, Lionetti (2014) reported that secure attachment in adopted infants is facilitated when mothers have secure attachment states of mind. In addition, Pace et al. (2019) reported that late-placed adopted adolescents showed both an increase in attachment security and a decrease in disorganized attachment from childhood to adolescence and that adoptive mothers' secure states of mind were significantly associated with their children' increase in attachment security in adolescence.

4.2 Adoption Communicative Openness

Among the many responsibilities of adoptive parents are sharing adoption information with their children, supporting their curiosity about their origins, helping them cope with adoption-related loss, promoting a positive view of their heritage, and supporting a positive sense of self and adoption identity. Success in achieving these tasks is linked to creating a family atmosphere that supports open communication about adoption, that involves sharing adoption information with children and sharing adoption-related feelings and becoming emotionally attuned to the children's adoption experiences (Brodzinsky, 2005).

Higher levels of communicative openness generally are associated with better psychological adjustment, including fewer behavior problems (Aramburu et al., 2020; Brodzinsky, 2006), more positive self-esteem (Brodzinsky, 2006; Hawkins et al., 2007), and more positive adoptive identity (Le Mare & Audet, 2011). In addition, communicative openness is related to more trust of adoptive parents by youth, fewer feelings of alienation from them, and better family functioning, as well as a greater effort to seek new information about their background as they enter young adulthood (Kohler et al., 2002). However, Grotevant et al. (2011) failed to find a relation between communicative openness and adolescents' psychological adjustment.

Not surprisingly, open adoptions that involve contact between adoptive and birth families are also associated with greater adoption communication between parents and children (Brodzinsky, 2006; Grotevant et al., 2011). Such contact leads to children asking more questions about birth family and the reasons for their adoption, thereby facilitating communication transactions between parents and children over time.

In short, when the adoptive family environment promotes an open and accepting atmosphere regarding conversations about adoption, and when adopted children and adolescents feel comfortable expressing their thoughts, feelings, and questions about adoption, they are much more likely to internalize their adoption experience in a positive manner and display positive psychological adjustment. This is especially true when parents foster what Reuter and Koerner (2008) describe as a *conversation orientation* that respects children's unique feelings and experiences about adoption and provides them with appropriate structure and guidance regarding important adoption issues such as helping to interpret background information, correcting misunderstandings about adoption, and supporting their search interests.

This style of communication contrasts with what the researchers referred to as a *conformity orientation,* in which parents engage in discussions about adoption with their children, but with an emphasis on promoting their own view of adoption experiences rather than respecting the unique experiences, perspectives, and interests of their adopted children. The distinction between conversation orientation and conformity orientation highlights the importance of recognizing that talking with children about adoption is not inherently the same as adoption communicative openness (Pinderhughes & Brodzinsky, 2019), an emotional and relational attitude that expresses parents' empathy and respect toward their children's needs and experiences (Brodzinsky, 2005).

4.3 Ethnic, Racial, and Cultural Socialization

As noted previously, over the past few decades, a growing percentage of adoptions involves transethnic, transracial, and/or transcultural placements, especially international adoptions, and those from domestic foster care. Among the many adoption-related responsibilities of parents in these types of adoption are supporting children's identity, self-esteem, pride, and adjustment in relation to their ethnicity, race, and cultural heritage through ethnic, racial, and cultural socialization (e.g., Ferrari & Rosnati, 2022; Pinderhughes & Brodzinsky, 2019). This aspect of parenting involves providing information, perspectives, experiences, and skills related to the child's ethnic, racial, and cultural origins. An important part of this socialization process is preparation-for-bias that is associated with ethnic, racial, and cultural minority status, including being part of a transracial, transethnic, and/or transcultural adoptive family. Because transracially adopted children and their families are often exposed to microaggression and microinsults (Zhang et al., 2019) as well as more overt forms of discrimination and bias, it is important for parents to help their children learn to navigate these experiences.

For adoptive parents to be successful in supporting children's ethnic, racial, and cultural identity and self-esteem, as well as their psychological adjustment, they must first acknowledge the importance of ethnicity, race, and culture in the family's life (especially the child's) as well as the reality of prejudice, bias, and stigma that is associated with ethnic/racial/cultural minority status in society. When parents readily acknowledge ethnic, racial, and cultural differences in the family, can see these differences from both their own and the child's perspectives, are aware of their own implicit biases and stereotypes related to these issues, recognize the importance of providing exposure to the child's ethnic, racial, and cultural origins, and value the importance of preparing children for stigma, they are more likely to provide ethnic, racial, and cultural socialization, including preparation-for-bias (Lee et al., 2006; Pinderhughes et al., 2015).

Successful socialization in these areas involves connecting children to their origins and redefining the family as one that is multiethnic, multiracial, or multicultural. As parents share information about the child's origins, they can also take the opportunity to talk about their own unique heritage, which is often different for parents, even those who are the same race (e.g., parents may come from different religious backgrounds or different cultural heritages). Such conversations reinforce the reality that children are not the only ones who are different in the family; that is, each member has a unique heritage that enriches the entire family.

Adoptive parents are highly variable in the extent to which they engage in these types of socialization practices as well as in the strategies they use. Some of the common strategies used by parents include: talking with children about their ethnic, racial, and cultural heritage; reading books with children that incorporate information about their heritage; attending activities or events that are related to children's heritage; developing friendships with families of color and other transracial adoptive families; finding an ethnic, racial, or cultural mentor for children; developing relationships with the child's birth relatives (when possible); and visiting the child's birth country (Pinderhughes & Brodzinsky, 2019).

Parents' success in engaging in heritage socialization depends, in part, on where they live. When families live in urban areas and multicultural countries, parents are often able to find appropriate resources to support ethnic, racial, and cultural socialization efforts. But when families live in small towns and rural areas, or in more ethnically/racially/culturally homogeneous countries, such resources are often limited, reducing opportunities for such socialization, and resulting in children and their families sometimes feeling marginalized in their communities. In addition, parents who more often have previous experiences interacting with minority group members, and who less often adopt a "color-blind" attitude, are more likely to expose their children to their ethnic, racial, and cultural heritage and prepare them for possible discrimination (Hrapczynski & Leslie, 2018). However, the tendency of adoptive parents to prepare their children for bias may vary depending on their children's ethnic, racial, or cultural heritage. For example, Killian and Khana (2019) reported that "color-conscious" parents of Black adopted children were more likely to prepare them for discrimination and bias than "color-conscious" parents of Asian and Latino adopted children.

Research has also focused on the impact of ethnic, racial, and cultural socialization on children's adjustment. Johnston et al. (2007), for example, reported that White mothers of Asian adopted children who engaged in more cultural socialization had children with fewer externalizing problems, but not internalizing problems. Racial and cultural socialization are also associated with decreased feelings of marginalization and increased self-esteem (Mohanty & Newhill, 2011) as well as with adoptees' ethnic identity and pride (Hu et al., 2015). Moreover, Rosnati and Ferrari (2014) noted that, whereas the perception of social discrimination undermined the ethnic identity of adolescent and young adult Italian adoptees, adoptive parents' cultural socialization strategies played a vital role in supporting their ethnic identity

Finally, there has also been a focus on bicultural socialization efforts by adoptive parents and its impact on transracial and transcultural adoptees. This aspect of socialization supports adoptees' connection to their birth culture and to their adoptive country. Manzi et al. (2014) noted that youth who receive cultural socialization in relation to their birth heritage are also more likely to feel connected to their adoptive parents' national identity. When adoptees are successful in integrating both aspects of their identities, they generally experience more positive well-being (Ferrari et al., 2015; Manzi et al., 2014). However, when they have difficulty integrating both their ethnic and national identities, they often feel "caught in the middle" and display greater adjustment difficulties (Manzi et al., 2014).

5 Emergence and Development of Adoptive Identity

"Who am I?" "Where do I fit in?" "How do I feel about myself and how do others view me?" These are just some of the questions that typically are addressed by people in the process of identity development. But for some individuals, this process is more complicated than for others. This is especially true for adopted individuals, who are inextricably linked to at least two families, the one that gave them life and the one that reared them.

The development of adoptive identity is all the more complex when one considers the different pathways to adoption (e.g., domestic infant placement; older child placement from foster care; intercountry placement), the varying degrees of information that adoptees have about their origins and the circumstances leading to their adoption, the diversity in the composition of adoptive families (e.g., same-race placement versus transracial placement), the different contexts in which the individual and family live (e.g., racially diverse society or community versus more racially homogeneous society or community), the diverse timing and intensity of the experience of adoption-related loss, and the varying degrees of openness within the adoptive family and between adoptive and birth families (Bornstein & Suwalsky, 2021; Grotevant & von Korff, 2011).

In short, answers for questions such as "Who am I as an adopted person and how do I feel about being adopted?," "Who are my birth parents, and to what extent am I similar to them?," "Do I have biological siblings and, if so, what happened to them?," and "How has being adopted impacted my life?" are influenced by a myriad of intersecting factors. Consequently, in their exploration of adoptive identity, researchers and scholars have been guided by several theoretical perspectives, including by not limited to: Erikson's psychosocial theory and narrative theories (Grotevant & Von Korff, 2011), ecological systems theory (Grotevant & Von Korff, 2011; Palacios, 2009), and cognitive developmental and stress and coping theories (Brodzinsky, 1990, 2011b). In the following sections, we explore how adoptive identity develops, including those individual and contextual factors that support or undermine a healthy and secure sense of self. We begin by examining the nature and implications of adoption-related loss for adoptees' identity and self-esteem.

5.1 Adoption-Related Loss and Identity Development

Common to all adopted individuals is the experience of loss and grief. Understanding the losses associated with adoption, learning to cope with them, processing adoption-related grief, and finding ways of integrating those experiences into their identity are critical development achievements for adoptees.

Loss in adoption is universal and pervasive (Brodzinsky, 2011b). Not only are adoptees separated from their birth parents, but also others in the birth family, including grandparents, uncles and aunts, cousins, and sometimes even siblings. For children placed very early in life, these family disruptions are seldom traumatic, primarily because attachments were never formed with these individuals. As children get older and begin to reflect on these individuals, however, it is common for them to experience a deep sense of loss related to relationships that were never allowed to form. For children removed from their birth family at older ages, separation from parents, siblings, and extended family is likely to be more disruptive and even traumatic because these individuals most often played significant roles in their lives, with some being important attachment figures, even when abuse and neglect were present. Older placed children also experience the loss of nonbiological support figures from the past, such as friends, teachers, and therapists. In addition, children adopted from foster care and those who experienced institutional life often form strong and meaningful relationships with caregivers and other children they lived with. The loss of these individuals can be quite disruptive for adoptees.

As children grow up, it is common for them to ask questions about their early years. "What was I like as a baby?" "Was I easy to care for or difficult?" When children continue to live with the people who reared them from infancy, these questions are easily answered. For adoptees who have been separated from their early caregivers (e.g., birth parents, foster parents, or institutional staff), these questions too often are unanswerable. The loss of a "meaning maker" (i.e., the person or people who can describe and explain the child's early years) leaves not only a long-lasting informational gap in the child's life narrative, but also an emotional void for the person's emerging identity.

At some point, children begin to recognize that most people view adoptive family status as "second-best" compared to growing up in the family of birth. French (2013) coined the term "birth privilege" to describe the inherent societal bias against which adopted individuals are often judged by others and themselves. This experience sometimes leads adopted children to feel "lesser than" their nonadopted peers, potentially underlying their self-esteem, identity, and adjustment. Because adopted individuals and their adoptive family members do not share a genetic link, it is also quite common that they look physically different or have different personality traits or abilities. For some children and adolescents, these differences can result in feelings of not "fitting in" or "belonging" to the family, yet another loss that can complicate identity and adjustment. This is especially true for adoptees who are placed across ethnic, racial, and/or cultural lines. Integrating adoption, ethnicity, race, culture, and other aspects of identity can be particularly challenging for these individuals when they live with families and/or in communities that do not offer them appropriate models, information, and experiences that help them understand what it means to be adopted and what it means to be a member of a particular ethnic, racial, or cultural group (Pinderhughes & Brodzinsky, 2019).

Coping with adoption-related loss and grief and integrating one's experiences into a healthy, secure, and cohesive adoptive identity can be challenging for several reasons. Because adoption is statistically uncommon in most societies (e.g., approximately 2 percent of children in the United States are adopted), adopted youth often feel that there are few people who truly understand what they are experiencing, which can accentuate feelings of being different and compromise self-esteem and identity. In addition, adoption loss is not necessarily permanent in some respects. Birth family members and other significant figures from the past are usually alive. Even when they are unknown and there is no contact with these individuals, they continue to live in the thoughts and emotional life of the adopted person (Brodzinsky, 2014), keeping fantasies of reunion a possibility. For some, these feelings are more intense than for others. The child's understanding of the reasons for adoptive placement can also make it difficult to integrate being adopted into a secure sense of self. When children understand that they were voluntarily placed for adoption by their birth parents, it can raise questions about whether they were unwanted because of characteristics or behaviors that the birth parents found unacceptable (e.g., "I cried too much"; "they didn't want a boy"). When children understand that they were removed from their birth parents by child welfare authorities, it can raise questions about whether they come from people who are damaged and whether they too will have similar problems as their birth parents. In either case, children can potentially internalize negative beliefs about themselves and their origins, undermining self-esteem and identity. Finally, adoption loss is often unrecognized by others, who tend to focus more on what the child has gained because of their adoptive placement. Such circumstances often result in adoptees feeling ignored, misunderstood, and unsupported, leading to what Doka (1989) referred to as "disenfranchised grief," which is much more difficult to resolve than when a person's grief is both acknowledged and supported.

In short, adoption loss and grief are universal for adoptees. Yet how these life experiences are understood by adopted children and the impact they have on self-esteem and identity depend on many factors, including the person's developmental level, the adoption information available to them, the parents' communication style, the support received from others, their propensity to explore adoption issues, and the salience of adoption in their emerging identity.

5.2 Developmental Perspectives on Adoptive Identity

Adoptive identity begins when children are first informed of their adoptive family status – typically through a simple and naïve story told to them in the preschool to early school years – and seek to understand its meaning. Although most children at this age can label themselves as "being adopted" and have developed a rudimentary adoption language (i.e., they can often recite a brief version of their adoption story shared by parents), they have little understanding of what adoption means (Brodzinsky, 2011b; Brodzinsky et al., 1984). It is not until middle childhood that adoptees possess the cognitive maturity and experience beyond the family to begin to appreciate the differences between adoption and birth as pathways to family membership. Adoption-related thoughts and feelings often emerge during this period and, unless there is a family atmosphere of open communication about adoption, the adoptive parents remain unaware of how their children are experiencing being adopted and sometimes believe that it is of little interest to or has minimal impact on their children. In addition, during adolescence and young adulthood, individuals develop a deeper cognitive and social understanding of adoption, including its legal status, differing social views and values about adoption, and the motivations and life circumstances underlying the reasons why people adopt children and why birth parents place their children for adoption or have their children removed from their care by child welfare authorities.

Although adoptive identity begins to develop when children first learn about their unique family status, it is, in fact, a lifelong journey involving the cyclical interweaving of multiple processes, including exploration, assessment, reconsideration, consolidation, and integration of information related to the self and one's relationship to others (Grotevant & von Korff, 2011). Even though there is a developmental course to building an adoption identity, it is not a linear process in which new phases supersede the previous ones. Thoughts and feelings about the unknown or the past may emerge later in life – for instance, during life transitions such as getting married, becoming a parent, or losing an adoptive parent. The desire to know more about the past or to initiate some contact with the birth family may be more salient in certain periods than in others. The outcome of these processes and life experiences is an emerging self-narrative or identity regarding being adopted that is constructed and reconstructed over time as individuals actively explore what they know about their history, how they feel about being adopted, what feedback they have received from others about adoption and the circumstances of their placement, what contact, if any, they have had with birth family members, the impact that contact has had on them, and what information they still desire but do not yet have about themselves.

There is considerable variability among adoptees in terms of their inclination to explore adoption-related issues, the centrality of adoption for their sense of self, and their feelings about self and being adopted (Colaner, 2014; Dunbar & Grotevant, 2004). Colaner (2014) has described two orthogonal dimensions that are part of the adoption identity process. *Reflective exploration* involves the degree to which adoptees think about their adoption and its meaning in their lives and *preoccupation* refers to the salience given to adoption as a component of the person's identity. High levels of preoccupation indicate that adoption is viewed not just as an important aspect of one's identity, but as one of the primary organizing perspectives through which the person explores and understands their self, and their relationships with others and the world (Grotevant et al., 2000).

The intersection of these two dimensions results in four distinct patterns of adoption identity, defined slightly differently by different researchers (Colaner, 2014; Dunbar & Grotevant, 2004; Grotevant et al., 2017). Individuals who display higher levels of reflective exploration, but relatively low to moderate levels of preoccupation are thought to have engaged in the most adoptive identity work and to have integrated adoption into their sense of self in a reasonably healthy and cohesive manner. Dunbar and Grotevant (2004) refer to these individuals as the *integrated* group. Others manifest high levels of reflective exploration, but also high levels of preoccupation, their identity work being considered still unresolved – these individuals are identified as the *unsettled* group by Dunbar and Grotevant (2004). Many of these individuals are actively searching for information about their adoption, including their original birth certificate (OBC) or access to their adoption files, but find themselves confronting obstacles in their adoption search process, resulting in great frustration (Rizzo Weller, 2022). The third group of adoptees display low levels of reflective exploration, but moderate to high levels of preoccupation in relation to adoption – described as having a *limited* adoptive identity by Dunbar and Grotevant (2004). Although adoption is salient for these individuals, they tend not to reflect on the reasons for its salience and the way in which it relates to other aspects of their identity. Sometimes the meaning of adoption they have internalized reflects others' views of adoption (e.g., their adoptive parents) rather than their own self-assessment of this identity issue. Finally, those adolescents described by Dunbar and Grotevant (2004) as being in the *unexamined* group present with both low adoption exploration and low preoccupation, suggesting little curiosity or effort to address the meaning of adoption in their lives and a sense of self that is relatively independent of their adoptive status. High levels of preoccupation in relation to adoption are often linked to low self-esteem (Horstmann et al., 2016), negative thoughts and feelings about adoption and birth parents (Colaner & Soliz, 2015), more adjustment issues (Grotevant et al., 2017), and more emotional distance from and lack of trust of adoptive parents (Kohler et al., 2002). High reflective exploration and low to moderate preoccupation is associated with higher levels of identification with both the adoptive and birth families (Colaner et al., 2018).

5.3 Family Influences on Adoptive Identity Development

Among the most important tasks for adoptive parents are sharing adoption information with their children and engaging them in adoption-related conversations (Pinderhughes & Brodzinsky, 2019). Parental attitudes and emotional tone associated with these tasks, as well as parents' willingness to initiate conversations and respond to children's curiosity and questions about adoption, are critical for creating a caregiving environment conducive to supporting adoptive identity exploration. To promote such exploration, adoptive parents must first acknowledge the unique aspects associated with adoptive family status that children inevitably confront as they develop, such as their inherent connection to two or more families, confusion about their origins and the reasons for their adoption, loss and grief related to separation from their birth family, and coping with differences between themselves and family members (e.g., in transracial placements). Unfortunately, some adoptive parents identify adoption communication only with discussions about known information, so that if there is little known about the child's past, there is little effort to engage children regarding their adoption experience. More importantly, not all parents find it easy to acknowledge the inherent differences associated with adoptive status, choosing instead to minimize or reject the differences and rearing their children as if they were born to them. Kirk (1964) suggested that this "rejection-of-difference" coping style created difficulties for adopted children because there was no emotional space in the family to address the differences they felt and the unanswered questions about adoption they had (Lo & Cashen, 2020).

The adopted person's need to explore their origins and the meaning of adoption in their life is both normal and inevitable (Müller & Perry, 2001), although as noted in Section 5.2, there is variability in the extent and emotional intensity to which such exploration is undertaken. There is a natural progression for most adoption searches. For children, the search begins with basic questions about where they come from, who their birth parents are, and why they were adopted. As they get older, there often is a desire to understand the origin of their physical characteristics, traits, and talents. A more direct link between searching and identity development is found in adolescence and emerging adulthood, when individuals actively seek new information about their origins, sometimes trying to repair emotional vulnerabilities associated with adoption-related loss and grief, as well as feelings of envy and jealousy that are connected to feelings of difference. For those who have never felt security in adoptive family relationships, the search can also reflect a longing for human connection and attachment. This sometimes leads to efforts to contact birth family members. For most adopted people, though, searching is also fundamentally a reflection of innate curiosity and a desire to resolve unanswered questions that are at the core of their adoption experience. As noted in Section 5.2, satisfaction with the search process is tied to a family environment that gives the adopted person permission and support to explore adoption-related issues. This is most likely to occur when parents create an open communicative atmosphere related to adoption (Brodzinsky, 2005; Wrobel et al., 2003).

For transracial and intercountry adoptees, there are more complex issues in identity development, as they seek to navigate the intersection of adoption, ethnicity, race, culture, and other factors influencing their emerging sense of self. Lee (2003) coined the term "transracial paradox" to describe the complications that transracial adoptees face. He noted that transracial adoptees benefit from privileges usually conferred to their parents as members of their country's racially dominant group (e.g., in the United States, non-Hispanic White parents of European origin), but are disadvantaged by the stigmas associated with being adopted (Baden, 2016; Ferrari et al., 2022), as well as being an ethnic or racial minority member (Sue et al., 2007) and/or an immigrant (Lee, 2003). Integrating all these factors into a healthy, cohesive, and balanced identity is influenced by parents' success in addressing these issues in family conversations, a process referred to as ethnic/racial/ cultural socialization (see previous discussion of this process in Section 4).

5.4 Societal and Social Influences on Adoptive Identity Development

Societal attitudes and values related to adoption play an important role in the lived experiences of adoptees. Although anthropological scholars have reported very positive views about adoption and less focus on biological parenting in some non-Western cultures (Bowie, 2004), most Western societies generally privilege family membership through birth over adoptive family membership (French, 2013), which can lead to feelings of stigma, difference, and not belonging among adoptees, potentially undermining a healthy and secure identity. Societal laws and practices related to adoption also play an important role in the ability of the person to integrate adoption into their emerging sense of self. In some countries, the person's OBC and other adoption documents are sealed by the court at the time of adoption and a new birth certificate is issued with only the adoptive parents listed on the form. Although this practice was begun with the idea that it protected the best interests of all parties, many adopted individuals, as well as adoption professionals, believe that access to these documents is important for resolving adoption issues and fostering a cohesive and integrated identity for adoptees (Rizzo Weller, 2022). In other countries, the OBC is not changed after adoption and the key for obtaining information about the birth family and the circumstances leading to adoption is access to the files kept in the archives of child protective services.

As noted previously, the practice of open adoption varies from country to country. Where it is practiced and supported, contact with birth family increases the person's knowledge about their origin, the circumstances surrounding their adoption, and access to people who can serve as models for a more complete sense of self (Grotevant, 2020). Open adoption also promotes more adoption-related communication among adoptive family members, which, in turn, facilitates adoptive identity development (Von Korff & Grotevant, 2011).

Another social context in which adopted children and adolescents receive feedback about adoption and which can impact adoptive identity is their peer group and people in the community. Although most adopted individuals report positive adoption experiences with their friends and others, they also acknowledge experiencing a variety of adoption microaggressions while growing up. Building on minority stress theory (Meyer, 2003) and research on social microaggressions related to marginalized groups (Sue, 2010), adoption researchers have identified a variety of microaggressions experienced by adopted individuals and adoptive parents (Baden, 2016; Garber & Grotevant, 2015). Many adoptees and adoptive parents report overly intrusive questions related to themselves and their family. This is especially true in transracial placements in which the physical dissimilarities between family members are obvious – for example, "Is that your real mother?"; "Is your husband Chinese?." These types of interactions with others can be awkward or embarrassing and undermine family members' sense of privacy regarding their adoption experience. In some cases, adoptees experience microassaults, which are more conscious and explicit efforts by someone to inflict emotional pain through adoption-related insults – for example, "Your real mother didn't want you . . . she just got rid of you"; "You're a bastard." Whatever the nature of the microaggressions, the intended or unintended outcome for adopted individuals is a recognition that others view them as different or disadvantaged, which can complicate and ultimately compromise a secure identity and positive sense of self.

Finally, although we have highlighted the considerable variability in adoptive identity exploration and the different developmental and contextual factors that support or undermine a healthy, well-integrated, and balanced sense of self, it is important to point out that the challenges experienced by adoptees in this aspect of development do not appear to compromise at least one aspect of identity – namely, self-esteem. Meta-analysis of eighty-eight studies found no differences in self-esteem between adopted children and adolescents compared to their nonadopted agemates (Juffer & van IJzendoorn, 2007). Moreover, this outcome was found for both same-race and different-race adoptive families. This finding adds to the earlier research reviewed suggesting that most adoptees are well within the normal range of development, despite encountering more than average adversity and challenges than their nonadopted counterparts.

6 Modern Adoptive Families

There have been many controversial changes in adoption practices over the years. Two that have generated considerable debate as well as a significant amount of research are open adoption and adoption by sexual minority individuals. In this section, we discuss the nature of these modern adoptive families and the controversies and research findings that have addressed them. Although these two possibilities exist in a growing number of countries, in some only one of them is possible and in others neither is allowed.

6.1 Open Adoption

As discussed in Section 1, adoption has a long history, with different priorities and practices during different time periods. Prior to the rise of the modern child welfare system in the early part of the twentieth century, when adoption was more informal and not yet institutionalized, it was common for birth parents to place their children with known families and to have some level of contact with them following placement (Baran & Pannor, 1990). This practice began to change with the emergence of public and (where they existed) private adoption agencies, which had government authority for placing in adoptive homes abandoned and vulnerable children, as well as children whose parents chose not to rear them. Independent and informal child placements were criticized by adoption agencies as not being in the best interests of adoptive kinship members. To protect the well-being of these individuals, agencies argued successfully that adoption placements needed to be closed, with no sharing of information or contact between the parties, either before or after adoption placement. In those cases when babies were abandoned and entered institutional care before being adopted, no efforts were made to register the circumstances and people involved, and therefore no identifying information could be shared. For nearly 50 years, the practice of closed or confidential adoptions went unchallenged.

In the 1970s and 1980s, however, perspectives on adoption practice began to change. In the United States, adult adoptees and birth parents, who had longed for information about one another, began to voice their concerns about the practices of closed adoptions, including sealing of the child's OBC and barriers to postplacement contact. Soon, a small group of adoption professionals suggested that some problems identified in adopted persons were a function of the inherent secrecy and stigmatization that are part of the closed adoption experience (Sorosky et al., 1975) and that open adoption should be standard practice (Baran & Pannor, 1993). Proponents of open adoption argued that eliminating secrecy in adoption was morally justified and would facilitate healthier adjustment in all adoptive kinship members. The arguments of these professionals, however, were met with resistance from many in the adoption community who believed that the philosophy and practice of open adoption would undermine the well-being of all members of the adoptive kinship system, especially the adopted child (Kraft et al., 1985). Although the path leading to open adoption was different in other countries, concerns about its negative impact were similar and confidential adoption was the norm.

In response to this debate, a substantial body of research has emerged over the past four decades, most of which has focused on domestic infant adoptions, although a smaller literature also exists on openness in foster care adoptions and international adoptions. To date, the findings have largely supported the benefits of open adoption compared to its potential drawbacks (Grotevant, 2020), although researchers and child welfare professionals have noted difficulties in some postadoption contact arrangements from foster care. Because of the benefits associated with open adoption, it is now being practiced in an increasing number of countries.

6.1.1 Dynamics and Patterns of Open Adoption

Several longitudinal studies have explored the dynamics and outcomes of open adoption arrangements outside of the United States (Neil et al., 2015, in England; Ward et al., 2022, in Australia), but the Minnesota Texas Adoption Research Project (MTARP), which has followed 190 US adoptive families and 169 birth mothers over 30 years, and through multiple waves of assessment, has been the pioneering effort in the field and produced the most information regarding the nature of open adoption and its impact on adoptive kinship members. This longitudinal project focuses on domestically adopted infants and their adoptive families who experienced different patterns of contact with the children's birth families from the time of placement to early adulthood (see Grotevant, 2020, for a summary of the MTARP).

Findings from this project indicate that the extent and nature of contact between members of the adoptive and birth families can change dramatically over time, with some previously closed adoptions opening and other adoptions that previously involved some level of contact closing down (Grotevant, 2020). Reasons for changes in the extent of contact between families are highly variable. Increased contact sometimes is the result of removal of legal barriers to birth and adoption records, allowing individuals to contact their birth families for the first time. In other cases, an adopted individual's life circumstances (e.g., birth of a child) stimulate an interest in finding out more about their own health history. In addition, as adolescents and young adults become more independent of their adoptive parents, growing curiosity to know more about their origins may stimulate a new desire, as well as a sense of freedom, to seek contact with their birth families. However, dissatisfaction with the extent, type, or quality of contact may lead some individuals, even those who had contact from the beginning of the adoption, to reduce or even end contact with the other family. In addition, contact may be lost in ways that are beyond the person's control, such as when one side abruptly ends communication or visits. Changes in the type of contact over time are also quite common. For example, contact that began as letters, emails, or through social media may shift to video visits or even face-to-face meetings as people get to know and trust one another and desire more direct involvement in each other's lives. Sometimes face-to-face meetings prove to be too inconvenient because of distance, and, consequently, subsequent contact may be primarily through indirect means such as emails, social media, or video chats. Discomfort with face-to-face visits, for whatever reason, can also lead the parties to choose more indirect means for future contact. In short, there are many reasons why contact between families may change over time, both in the extent and type of contact (Grotevant et al., 2019).

Based on emotional distance regulation theory, Grotevant (2009) described the unique dynamics involved in adoptive and birth families establishing, maintaining, and coping with contact with one another. He noted that these individuals bring to their interactions unique developmental histories, relationship expectations, expectations about adoption, and relationship skills that influence the creation of contact plans and their satisfaction with contact over time. In addition, he described several strategies that adoptive and birth family members use to comfortably regulate emotional distance among themselves, leading to more satisfying open adoption arrangements, including: (a) establishing clear boundaries related to decision-making, the nature of visits, and respective roles in relation to the child; (b) maintaining respect for one another and recognizing the unique contributions that each brings to relationships with the child; (c) providing support to each other, especially in times of difficulty; (d) tolerating the ambiguity and complexity involved in open adoption relationships; and (e) allowing interfamilial relationships to grow slowly over time as a way of building mutual understanding, empathy, and trust. Some of these processes are similar to those described by Neil et al. (2015), who highlighted the importance of how the adults involved think about and manage contact in foster care adoptions.

Although contact often varies over time and is influenced by many personal, interpersonal, and contextual factors, Grotevant and his colleagues (Dunbar & Grotevant, 2004; Grotevant et al., 2019) identified four discrete contact patterns among the families studied. In some cases, there was consistently no contact between the two families ("no-contact group"); for others, contact began but then ended at some point ("stopped contact group"); a third group involved families that had ongoing contact with one another, but was limited in its extent, frequency, and/or means ("limited contact group"); and a fourth group had ongoing contact over time involving multiple members of each family and through multiple means ("extended contact group"). A primary focus of these researchers, as well as other research teams, has been studying the impact of open adoption on adoptive kinship members.

6.1.2 Impact of Open Adoption

Although contact between adoptive and birth families certainly creates personal and relationship complexities for individuals in both families, and, at times, uncertainty about the benefits of such an arrangement, research has generally found more positive than negative consequences for open adoptions. For example, contact with the birth family is associated with increased curiosity and questions about adoption on the part of children and teenagers, which in turn facilitates more adoption-related family conversations and results in adopted individuals gaining information about themselves and their origins and developing a better understanding of adoption (Wrobel & Dillon, 2009; Wrobel & Grotevant, 2019). In addition, children and adolescents who have contact with birth parents report higher satisfaction with their contact status than those who do not have contact (Mendenhall et al., 2004). Adoptees' satisfaction with contact status has also been linked with more sensitive and open communication about adoption with their parents and with more secure attachments with them (Farr et al., 2014). The extent of contact with birth family members is not related to adopted individuals' psychological adjustment during childhood and adolescence (Brodzinsky, 2006; Ge et al., 2008; Von Korff et al., 2006), whereas satisfaction with contact status is associated with more positive adjustment (Grotevant et al., 2011). Beyond childhood, those young adults who experienced sustained high levels of contact and satisfaction with contact over time (extended contact group) reported lower levels of psychological distress and higher levels of psychological well-being than individuals who experienced increased, but limited, contact over time (limited contact group). No differences were found in adjustment between the extended contact group and those individuals who experienced no contact with birth family and those who experienced contact that stopped at some point in time (Lo et al., 2023). This finding implies that, although important, the impact of level of contact needs to be considered together with other factors associated with adoptees' adjustment.

Adoptive parents also appear to benefit from open adoption. Grotevant et al. (1994) reported that adoptive parents involved in open arrangements manifested the least fear about the birth parents' desire to reclaim their child, whereas those in the no-contact group expressed the greatest fear of this possibility. In addition, when their children were in adolescence, adoptive parents who had ongoing contact with the birth family expressed greater satisfaction with their contact status than those who had no contact with the birth family (Grotevant et al., 2011).

Open adoptions involving foster care placements are more complicated. These types of adoptions typically involve children removed from their families because of neglect, abuse, or other parent and family difficulties. In these circumstances, postadoption contact between children and their birth family has often been viewed as inconsistent with the child's and adoptive family's well-being. And yet, there has been increasing consideration given regarding the circumstances under which postadoption contact for children placed from foster care could be in their best interests (Boyle, 2017; Neil et al., 2015), especially regarding contact with siblings living elsewhere (Meakings et al., 2021). In the Australian state of New South Wales, postadoption contact is required by law in all adoptions (Ward et al., 2022). The rationale for postadoption contact from foster care is that it will support continuation of existing relationships with birth family members, foster a better understanding for the child of the circumstances leading to their adoptive placement, and facilitate a more complete, secure, and coherent identity. Existing evidence suggests that such contact can be quite beneficial for some, but not all, children (Boyle, 2017). Positive postadoption contact is most likely to occur when a collaborative and mutually respectful relationship has been established between the adoptive and birth families, whereas negative postadoption contact experiences more likely occur for children who have ongoing contact with birth parents who previously abused them. The bottom line is that contact following adoption from foster care must be decided on a case-by-case basis, with the primary focus of case planning being on the child's safety and emotional interests.

Contact between adoptive and birth families in international adoptions is also more difficult because of adverse circumstances leading to adoption (e.g., abandonment, extreme poverty, neglect, maltreatment), geographical distance, language and cultural/legal barriers, inadequate record keeping by authorities in sending countries, and, at times, resistance to contact by adoptive parents, who may have chosen international adoption over domestic adoption as a way of avoiding contact with birth family. And yet there is evidence that internationally placed adoptees and their families are searching for and at times contacting birth families (Brodzinsky & Goldberg, 2017; Koskinen & Böök, 2019; Tieman et al., 2008). Given the growing acceptance of search and reunion within the adoption community, the worldwide availability of the internet and social media, and the growing availability of DNA testing, it is reasonable to expect that contact between internationally adopted individuals and their birth families will grow over time.

6.2 Adoption by Sexual Minority Adults

More and more sexual minority adults are becoming parents through adoption. Like in other areas of sexual minority parenting (Bos & Gartrell, 2020; Tasker & Lavender-Stott, 2020), this development has been met with questions as to whether adopted children are disadvantaged when reared by lesbian or gay parents and whether these parents manifest different characteristics or parenting qualities than their heterosexual counterparts. In this section, we address these questions, as well as trends and practices in adoption by lesbians and gay men.

6.2.1 Trends and Practices in Adoption by Sexual Minority Adults

Adoption has become an increasingly popular pathway to parenthood for sexual minority adults in many Western countries (Farr et al., 2020). According to Equaldex,[1] an online collaborative knowledge base that collects and analyzes data about LGBT laws, facts, and opinions globally, by region and country, as of 2022, fifty-four countries have laws allowing same-sex couples to adopt. In another 125 regions, the ability of lesbians and gay men to adopt is described as "somewhere in between," with the possibility of single-parent adoptions in many regions. It is unclear, however, what percentage of single-parent adoptions in these regions involves individuals who openly identify to the authorities as lesbian or gay. Finally, in forty-one countries adoption by sexual minority adults remains illegal.

Most children adopted by sexual minority adults involve either domestic private placement by their birth parents, where this practice exists (e.g., in the United States), when the children are still infants, or through the country's public foster care system when children usually are older and often have medical, mental health, and/or educational special needs. In domestic private adoptions, some birth parents show a preference for having their children placed with sexual minorities (Brodzinsky, 2011a; Farr et al., 2022). Reasons for this preference are varied and include a positive history with sexual minority individuals; a desire to place with individuals who cannot have a biologically related child; a desire to have an open adoption, which is often supported by lesbians and gay men; and for some birth mothers placing with gay men in an open adoption, the desire to be their child's only mother.

Placement of children with sexual minority individuals through foster care is typically determined by the adoption authorities, with little control by the child's birth parents. In such cases, the law, the agency's policies, and the attitudes of caseworkers determine whether sexual minority clients are judged as suitable for an adoption placement. In fewer cases, sexual minority individuals and couples seek to adopt children from other countries, but must do so without openly identifying themselves as LGBT because virtually all sending countries do not permit placement of their children with such persons (Brodzinsky, in press). Adoption agencies that facilitate intercountry placements with sexual minority individuals often adopt a "don't ask, don't tell" policy, and submit the home study paperwork and other adoption documents without identifying the prospective parents as lesbian or gay. But in doing so, they face an ethical dilemma. In facilitating intercountry adoption placements with LGBT individuals, agencies are prioritizing the needs of vulnerable children who desperately need a safe, stable, and nurturing home, as well as the needs of their adoption clients, over the

---

[1] www.equaldex.com/issue/adoption; accessed April 7, 2023.

laws, regulations, and customs of the child's birth country that they are supposed to abide by. The bottom line is that intercountry adoption by LGBT adults is complex, and there has been very little discussion about the most appropriate ways of confronting the ethical and practice issues involved.

Even when the law permits adoption by sexual minority adults, research has shown that these individuals frequently report discrimination, bias, and delays in their efforts to adopt children (Brodzinsky, 2011a; Goldberg, et al., 2019). In some cases, discrimination is based on the religious affiliation and beliefs associated with the adoption agency or on the prejudicial beliefs of adoption caseworkers, attorneys, or judges (Brodzinsky, 2011a). Despite these obstacles, sexual minority adults are highly motivated to become parents through adoption and in the United States adopt proportionately at higher rates than heterosexual adults (Gates, 2013). Sexual minority adults are disproportionately more likely to adopt racial minority children and frequently adopt children with developmental and emotional difficulties (Farr et al., 2020; Goldberg & Smith, 2009). In addition, they have been found to support contact between their children and birth families, sometimes even more than heterosexual parents (Brodzinsky & Goldberg, 2016, 2017; Goldberg, 2019).

6.2.2 Outcomes for Children Adopted by Sexual Minority Parents

Both cross-sectional and longitudinal studies have found few, if any, significant differences in psychological and behavior adjustment of adopted children as a function of parents' sexual orientation (see Farr et al., 2020, for a review). An exception to this pattern was reported in a UK study by Golombok et al. (2014) focusing on adopted children aged 3–9 years. Parent ratings of externalizing symptoms, but not internalizing symptoms, were higher in children of heterosexual parents than gay or lesbian parents. No group differences were found for teacher ratings of adjustment. A follow-up study of the same sample, when the children were between 10 and 14 years, found no differences in children's psychological adjustment as a function of parents' sexual orientation (McConnachie et al., 2021). Although parents' sexual orientation was generally unrelated to adopted children's adjustment in these studies, several parent variables were significantly associated with patterns of adjustment for all family types, including quality of parenting, parents' mental health, parental stress, and couple conflict (Farr, 2017; Goldberg & Smith, 2013; McConnachie et al., 2021). These results reinforce research suggesting that family structure is less important for children's well-being than family processes (Golombok, 2015).

Gender development has also been studied for children adopted by sexual minority parents. Using both parent-report and observational data, Farr et al.

(2018) found no substantive differences in gender-related play and activities as a function of parents' sexual orientation. In contrast, Goldberg and Garcia (2016) reported less gender-stereotyped play in children of sexual minority parents compared to children of heterosexual parents, which could be due to more flexible attitudes about gender activities among sexual minority parents. Finally, few substantive differences have been found in quality of parenting and couple relationships between sexual minority parents and their heterosexual counterparts (Farr et al., 2020).

In summary, despite the resistance to adoption by sexual minority adults, which continues to exist in many countries, research suggests these individuals are highly motivated to rear adopted children, including those with special needs and who are racial minorities. As a result, these individuals should be viewed as valuable parenting resources for the thousands of children who continue to wait for family permanency through adoption.

7 Postadoption Family Needs, Supports, and Services

Given the greater numbers of older, ethnic and racial minority, and special needs children being placed for adoption today, as well as more children having contact with birth family members, there is a critical need for comprehensive preadoption parent preparation and assessment (Beesley, 2020; Brodzinsky, 2008; Lee et al., 2018) and well developed and accessible postadoption services and supports for all family members (Lee et al., 2020; Merritt & Ludeke, 2020). Moreover, because adoption is a lifelong journey, the need for postadoption services and support goes beyond those that are provided to families soon after adoptive placement, or even those that are available during the child's developing years. Indeed, the need for services and support appears to increase over time (Wind et al., 2007). In addition, research on adoption disruption and breakdown has consistently shown that readily available services and support for adoptive families are crucial for ensuring the stability of adoptive placements (Palacios, Rolock, et al., 2019). In this section, we explore issues related to the different types of postadoption needs manifested by family members, the support and services that are commonly available and utilized by them, the barriers to accessing the services, and the effectiveness of these services, especially parenting interventions, for meeting the needs of adoptive parents in rearing their children.

7.1 Types of Postadoption Services and Support

There are many types of services and support available to adoptive parents and their children (Merritt & Ludeke, 2020; Penner, 2023), with types and availability differing by country or even by state or region within countries. Some services focus primarily on providing emotional support to family members (e.g., parent and child support groups, individual and family counseling); others are more informational or skill building in nature (e.g., online adoptive parent courses, parent education classes, referral hotlines and information networks, academic tutoring for children); some focus on advocacy training for parents with service providers, schools, and other professionals who do not adequately understand the child's or family's needs; still others focus on stabilizing families during a crisis (e.g., crisis counseling, parent respite care). Finally, depending on the type of adoption and where it takes place, other support provides families with access to adoption subsidies offered by child welfare agencies that pay for medical and mental health care for children, out-of-pocket childcare expenses, and/or home modifications and vehicle equipment to support special needs children.

Postadoption services and support are invaluable for meeting the needs of adopted children and their parents. Use of postadoption services is associated with decreased emotional and behavioral problems in children and more effective and satisfactory parenting as well as decreased likelihood of adoption instability or breakdown (Palacios, Rolock, et al., 2019; Smith & Howard, 1999). Although efforts to assess the effectiveness of postadoption services have been hampered by a lack of rigorous methodology and the heterogeneity of services offered to adoptive families (Penner, 2023), overall there is general agreement that adoptive families benefit from them.

Where they exist, adoption subsidies, as one key form of postadoption support, have had a profound effect on adoptive families, especially those adopting children from foster care. In the past, foster children too often lingered in care, without the benefit of a permanent family, undermining their emotional well-being compared to those who were adopted (Hjern et al., 2019). To meet the needs of these vulnerable children, the US Congress in 1980 passed a law that, for the first time, created a program of financial and medical assistance that helped promote adoption from foster care, reduced the financial burden of adoption, and allowed parents to meet the needs of children adopted from state care. The success of the adoption subsidy program can be seen in the large number of US children adopted from foster care since the passage of this legislation. Since 2010, over 50,000 children have been adopted from foster care each year.[2] Moreover, higher adoption subsidies have been associated with more stable adoption placements (Barth & Berry, 1990).

One aspect of postadoption support that has not received sufficient attention is parent self-care. Rearing adopted children can be extremely challenging,

---

[2] www.acf.hhs.gov/cb/research-data-technology/statistics-research/afcars.

especially for those individuals whose children are older at the time of placement and/or have significant medical, psychological, or educational special needs. High levels of stress and feelings of isolation are common among these parents (Atkinson & Gonet, 2007), especially when they do not have access to postadoption support (Santos-Nunes et al., 2018). Child welfare and mental health professionals clearly need to focus more on providing adoptive and foster families with strategies for stress reduction and health promotion, especially for those who are rearing special needs children.

Despite the many types of postadoption support and services available, adoptive parents often have difficulty accessing them or simply do not use them. In many cases, parents do not know what services are available to them or which ones they are eligible for (Dhami et al., 2007). Furthermore, those living in small towns or in rural areas may find that the services are not provided locally. In other cases, parents cannot afford the services, especially those provided by private agencies or mental health professionals. In other cases, parents may be reluctant to utilize postadoption services, believing that doing so reflects some level of failure on their part. A key factor in postadoption service use by adoptive parents is effective preadoption preparation (Brodzinsky, 2008; Wind et al., 2007). Those preparing and counseling adoptive parents must ensure that the message to their clients is that help-seeking, when it is needed, is a sign of strength and not an indication of parenting failure.

In short, there is a wide range of postadoption services available for adoptive families and clear evidence that the availability and utilization of these services benefit all family members, foster greater family cohesion, and support adoption stability (Penner, 2023). Despite this fact, too many families do not have access to these services or in some cases are reluctant to utilize them. Adoption professionals must make greater efforts to address these issues to support these vulnerable families, preventing adoption instability and breakdown (Palacios, Rolock, et al., 2019).

7.2 Factors Associated with Postadoption Needs and Service Use

Postadoption service and support needs are associated with many factors. Lee et al. (2020) highlighted characteristics associated with adoption type, as well as child and parent characteristics, that are linked to the adoptive family's postadoption needs and service use.

The child's pathway to adoption results in different types of postadoption needs. For example, in countries where domestic private agencies exist, like in the United States, children placed from foster care and from other countries are more likely to experience early adversities and traumas, as well as be older at the time of placement, than children placed from such agencies (Howard et al., 2004). These types of circumstances increase the risks for mental health and behavioral problems as well as difficulties adjusting to an adoptive placement. Helping parents understand the impact of preadoption adversity on their children, as well as the best strategies to support their children's recovery from traumatic experiences, is an important part of adoptive parent preparation and postadoption interventions to support placement stability and the well-being of all family members.

As discussed in Section 6.1, open adoptions involving some level of post-placement contact between adoptive and birth families are increasingly common in many countries. Adoptive parents are often unsure about the benefits and risks associated with open adoptions, especially when their children have experienced adversities at the hands of birth family members, and, consequently, sometimes find it useful to consult with adoption professionals regarding strategies for navigating the additional challenges associated with open adoption arrangements.

A variety of characteristics associated with children have also been linked to postadoption service needs. Children who experienced significant preplacement deprivation, abuse, and other traumas often enter their adoptive families with medical problems, such as growth deficiencies, neurological complications, precocious puberty, and developmental delays (Mason et al., 2014). These health difficulties can be daunting for adoptive parents and require the support of medical professionals, especially those well versed in the complications associated with preadoption life adversities. Many of these children also have learning challenges, requiring special education services, as well as psychological and behavioral problems that benefit from skilled mental health clinicians, especially those who are adoption clinically competent (Atkinson, 2020). Because children who are older at the time of placement typically have experienced more preadoption adversity, parents considering adopting these youngsters must be prepared for the probability of greater postplacement support needs. Children's current age is also a factor in postadoption service needs and use. As children get older, their developmental needs often become more complicated. The average child age at which parents first seek help is 12 years, suggesting that the transition to adolescence is a period of increased challenge for parents (Waid & Alewine, 2018), as research on adoption breakdown also shows (Palacios, Rolock, et al., 2019). In Western countries, many domestic and intercountry adoptions involve children placed across ethnic, racial, and cultural lines. These types of adoptions can present parents and their children with many challenges. As previously discussed, parents often need counseling and guidance for understanding different ethnic, racial, and cultural socialization strategies for their children as a means for supporting positive self-esteem and identity, as well as helping children cope with ethnic, racial, and cultural discrimination (Pinderhughes & Brodzinsky, 2019).

Parent demographics have also been linked to postadoption service needs and use. Higher levels of family income and parent education are associated with greater help-seeking (Zima et al., 2000), whereas lower education is linked to greater unmet service needs (Zwaanswijk et al., 2006). Finally, sexual minority parents who adopt children also benefit from postadoption supports related to helping their children understand and adjust to having same-sex parents and developing coping strategies to deal with homophobic comments and behavior by others (Battalen et al., 2019).

7.3 Parenting Interventions Addressing Postadoption Problems

Given that a sizable percentage of adoptions today involve children with adverse histories that result in difficulties in adjusting to their adoptive family, including trauma symptoms and complications in forming secure parent-child attachments, there has been significant efforts by professionals to develop clinical interventions to help adoptive and foster parents become more sensitive and competent caregivers and to facilitate more secure parent-child attachments and healthier child outcomes (Rushton & Monck, 2009; Waterman et al., 2018). A meta-analytic review of parenting interventions in adoption and foster care was reported by Schoemaker et al. (2020). A wide range of intervention programs and methodologies was represented in these studies. Eight meta-analyses were performed to assess the effectiveness of parenting interventions on four parent outcomes (i.e., sensitive parenting; dysfunctional discipline; parents' knowledge and attitudes about their child; parenting stress), one place-ment outcome (stability versus disruption), and three child outcomes (i.e., attachment security; behavior problems; diurnal cortisol levels). Effectiveness of parenting interventions varied for different outcome measures.

Parenting interventions were effective for all four parent outcome measures, significantly improving sensitive parenting and parents' knowledge and atti-tudes about their child, and reducing dysfunctional discipline strategies and parenting stress, compared to the control group. Only interventions targeting sensitive parenting, however, yielded a large effect size. Improvements in sensitive parenting were greater for individuals rearing children with challen-ging behavior problems compared to those whose children manifested fewer difficulties. In addition, group interventions resulted in greater improvement in sensitive parenting than individual interventions, suggesting that parents benefit more from going through such interventions with other adoptive and/or foster parents than from receiving them alone. This finding is consistent with other research indicating that group support from other adoptive parents is a valuable postadoption experience, fostering more effective parenting strategies, reduced stress (Viana & Welsh, 2010), and diminished likelihood of adoption dissolution (Hartinger-Saunders et al., 2015).

Parenting interventions did not impact placement disruption rates, although the influence of interventions on this outcome may not be a direct one. According to the authors, these interventions likely have an indirect effect on placement stability through their influence on parenting and child outcomes. As parenting quality improves and children's behavior becomes less challenging, placement disruption is likely to be reduced. Because it takes time for parent and child outcomes to improve through interventions, the impact on placement stability can be expected to be delayed beyond the intervention time frames used in the studies.

Meta-analyses of parenting interventions on child outcome data found a positive effect for reducing children's behavior problems, but not for improving their attachment security or impacting their diurnal cortisol levels. According to Shoemaker et al. (2020), the impact of parenting interventions on child outcomes is also likely indirect and results from changes in parenting behaviors, knowledge and attitudes, and stress level that interact with children's behavior. Because most of the parenting interventions in the studies reviewed occurred over relatively short time periods (four months, on average), changes in parenting outcomes may not have had a chance to impact child outcomes over this period.

Shoemaker et al. (2020) also suggested that the heterogeneity of the intervention strategies represented across the studies may have obscured specific types of interventions that are effective in changing specific child outcomes. Their conclusion is supported by research that was specifically designed to address children's attachment problems. For example, Zeegers et al. (2020) examined the impact of enhancing adoptive parents' sensitivity and mind-mindedness on children's attachment security, behavior problems, and parenting stress, characteristics that in past research were shown to be significantly associated with variations in children's attachment security, socio-emotional development, and/ or behavior problems (Colonnesi et al., 2019; Zeegers et al., 2018). In the study, the Basic Trust video feedback intervention model (see Colonnesi et al., 2013) was employed with fifty-three Dutch adoptive families with internationally adopted children, ages 2–12 years. Pretest, posttest, and 6-month follow-up assessments were conducted. The intervention was associated with significant improvement in fathers' and mothers' mind-mindedness, from pretest to posttest, and their sensitivity, from pretest to the 6-month follow-up. Improvement in mind-mindedness preceded improvement in sensitivity, suggesting that the intervention first changed parents' cognitions and perceptions of the child, after which changes in their behavior took place (i.e., sensitive responding). In addition, the intervention was associated with a positive impact on children's outcome measures, resulting in fewer child behavior problems and insecure and disorganized attachment at both the posttest and follow-up assessments.

The point noted above by Shoemaker et al. (2020) is also supported by video-feedback research aimed at fostering parental sensitive responding to children using the Positive Parenting and Sensitive Discipline (VIPP-SD) intervention (Juffer et al., 2008). A recent meta-analysis of twenty-five randomized controlled trials (RCTs) using VIPP-SD interventions, involving more than 2,000 parents and caregivers from a wide range of families, including two studies focusing on adoptive families and two on foster families, showed significant promotion of sensitive parenting behavior and attitudes, as well as increased security in child–parent attachment, but no reduction of children's externalizing behavior (van IJzendoorn et al., 2023). According to the authors, the failure of VIPP-SD to impact children's externalizing behavior is likely the result of their greater distal relationship compared to the more proximal relationship between the intervention and parenting behavior. In short, it simply takes more time for the VIPP-SD intervention to impact children's behavior.

It is clear that postadoption parenting interventions are a valuable resource for adoptive families, improving their parenting sensitivity, knowledge, and skills that facilitate better adjustment for children and more stable adoption placements. When professionals are not only skilled clinicians, experienced in working with traumatized and attachment impaired children, but also knowledgeable about the vicissitudes of adoption, they are able to support parents in helping their children recover from preadoption adversity and support them in managing the normative challenges of adoptive family life, such as talking with children about adoption, supporting their curiosity about their origins, and, for some, supporting contact with the birth family. Clinicians with these skills are considered to be adoption clinically competent (Atkinson, 2020; Riley & Singer, 2020).

8 Conclusions and Future Directions for Research, Practice, and Policy

There has been enormous progress made by adoption researchers in their attempts to disentangle the many complexities of adoptive family life as well as the lived experiences of being adopted. In the wake of our previous review of adoption research (Palacios & Brodzinsky, 2010), the current one highlights significant advances in research interests, theories, methods, and findings. Our understanding of adopted children, their life trajectories, and their families is completer and more integrative than ever before.

Research findings summarized in this Element are of clear interest for all those interested in adoption, but they also inform our understanding of human development through the very special circumstances associated with adoption, including: (a) separation of genetic and rearing influences; (b) the sharp discontinuity between early adverse life circumstances and the postadoption rearing environment; (c) development outside of the traditional biological family; and (d) the complexities in identity development. For example, adoption research has contributed to an understanding of how environmental circumstances moderate the impact of genetic influences on developmental trajectories (Reiss et al., 2023); it has contributed to a better awareness of the impact of early adversity and trauma on children's behavior and adjustment, as well as conditions that facilitate or hinder recovery from previous life difficulties (Brodzinsky et al., 2022; van IJzendoorn & Juffer, 2006); it has supported the views that children are not inherently disadvantaged when they are reared outside of their biological family and that family processes, such as quality of parenting, are more important for their health and well-being than family structure (Golombok, 2015); and it has fostered a better understanding of the complexities of identity development among individuals growing up in diverse family constellations and those subjected to minority group stigma and bias (Grotevant & Von Korff, 2011; Sue, 2010). Adoption researchers are encouraged to reflect on the implications of their findings not only for adoption, but also for the broader issues addressed in developmental science.

Just as we do not have a unified theory of human development, there is also no unified theory of adoption adjustment. In both cases, the domains and subdomains involved are too numerous, too complex, and too diverse to be captured by a single theory. However, integrative efforts inspired by such inclusive approaches as the bioecological model (Palacios, 2009) and the specificity principle of adoption (Bornstein & Suwalsky, 2021) are promising frameworks for understanding the many pieces of the puzzle that compose adoption adjustment. Hopefully, future scholars will build on these and other efforts to develop more integrative approaches to adoption theory and research.

The emergence of a greater number of longitudinal studies, some focusing on domestic adoption (Grotevant et al., 2017; Nadeem et al., 2017; Paine et al., 2021; Reiss et al., 2023) and others on intercountry adoption (Román et al., 2022; Sonuga-Barke et al., 2017) has contributed a rich source of knowledge about the lived experiences of adoptees and the dynamics of adoptive family life. Importantly, they have provided valuable information about the way adoption influences the person and the family over time, including the transactional relation between children and their parents. In some cases, these studies have incorporated a transdisciplinary approach, integrating theories and methods from different academic fields (e.g., genetic, neuroscience, psychology, social work), which further enriches our understanding of the complexities and nuances of adoption. We believe that the community of adoption researchers coming from different disciplinary domains is a key component to ensure a more comprehensive and integrated picture of adoption.

Another important change in adoption research is the frequent use of meta-analyses to examine patterns of findings across numerous studies assessing different areas of adoption adjustment (Askeland et al., 2017; Juffer & van IJzendoorn, 2005; Lionetti et al., 2015; Scott et al., 2011; van IJzendoorn & Juffer, 2006) and adoptive parenting (Schoemaker et al., 2020). Although not without its own limitations, meta-analysis provides an integrative perspective of relations between target variables and avoids some of the methodological limitations inherent in any individual study. Similar to our previous analysis of adoption research trends, topics, and findings (Palacios & Brodzinsky, 2010), there have also been recent efforts to provide critical and integrative reviews of different topics related to adoption adjustment such as disciplinary origins, methodological approaches, and theories used in addressing adoption issues (Séguin-Baril & Saint-Jacques, 2023), links between attachment and trauma (Fonagy et al., 2023), postadoption adjustment factors (Duncan et al., 2021), and postadoption services (Penner, 2023). Meta-analyses provide useful quantitative information about patterns of adoption adjustment, but review articles are more useful for their contextual analysis of research findings and theoretical concepts, their ability to reveal gaps in existing literature, and their value in pointing out implications of existing research for future empirical investigations, as well as for adoption policy and practice.

Bornstein and Suwalsky's (2021) introduction of the specificity principle of adoption also has implications for important methodological lessons for researchers. For example, researchers sometimes use subject samples that are heterogeneous with regard to potentially relevant child or parent characteristics (e.g., children's age, race, and age at adoption; parents' socioeconomic status) or adoption experiences (e.g., contact experiences with birth family) and fail to acknowledge that the results of the study may not generalize to subgroups within their sample (e.g., the results may be valid for those who have contact with birth family but not for those without such contact). Similarly, methods of data collection must be considered in drawing conclusions about the research findings. For example, data collected from one specific source (e.g., parents) may lead to different conclusions than data collected from a different source (e.g., children or teachers), and specific methods of data collection (e.g., self-report questionnaires) may lead to different conclusions than other types of data (e.g., observations of research participants). In short, the specificity principle of adoption emphasizes that conclusions drawn from research must consider numerous adoption specificities related to, among other factors, the pathway to adoption, where and when the adoption occurs, the experiences encountered prior to and during the adoption, the sociodemographics of participants, the various processes that potentially moderate the experience of adoption for all individuals involved, and the methods of data collection. Future researchers are encouraged to consider the implication of the specificity principle in designing and implementing their studies, and in the conclusions and implications drawn from their findings.

If adoption was once seen through rose-colored glasses, as an easy solution for the plight of vulnerable children whose biological parents could not or would not provide for them, the findings reported in this Element show a more complex reality. Even when the experience of adoption is successful and satisfactory for family members (which happens in most, but not all cases), adopted children and their parents are usually confronted with significant challenges in the face of children's efforts, with parental support, to recover from past adversities and in their attempts to construct a healthy, well-integrated personal and social identity. The experience of individuals touched by adoption and the research findings summarized here have made us more aware of the many complexities and challenges involved in achieving these important developmental tasks. In short, not minimizing adoption difficulties is as important as not pathologizing adoption.

In the face of the magnitude and complexity of the difficulties faced by many adoptive families, models of preventive and therapeutic interventions are critically important. Superficial and sporadic professional interventions, provided by child welfare workers or mental health professionals who are inadequately trained to address the difficulties faced by adoptive family members, are simply unacceptable. There is growing recognition among adoption scholars of the need for evidence-based interventions and support, provided by adoption-competent professionals who understand and can help resolve the specific problems of adopted persons and their families (Atkinson, 2020; Brodzinsky, 2013; Riley & Singer, 2020). Professional interventions (e.g., preadoption parent preparation; adoption suitability assessment; postadoption clinical, educative, and advocacy support) need to be tailored to the new realities of adoption, guided by the wealth of knowledge from adoption research and developmental science, and with an appreciation for the many specificities that characterize the adoption experience (Bornstein & Suwalsky, 2021). To serve the needs of those involved, readily available and cost-effective quality interventions must be offered. In addition, new possibilities have emerged for professionally guided support through live, online consultations with adoption clinical experts, adoptive parent education courses, and adoption-related webinars, as well as archived material on adoption. Online adoptive parent groups also provide a source of practical information and emotional support for parents. These new opportunities make training and support available for most adoptive families, regardless of where they live.

In terms of implications for policy, adoption numbers are on the decline in many countries. This is good news if it implies that more children are now finding their rights and needs met in their birth families, communities, and countries, which is the primary goal of protective services for children at risk. However, it is not good news if it implies that children who should be separated from their birth families because of chronic neglect, abuse, or other dangerous conditions, remain in unacceptable or unstable circumstances during childhood, and then confront an unsupported and difficult transition to adulthood and independence. Although birth family stabilization and family reunification efforts are always, and should be, the priority in child welfare, better efforts must be made to ensure that children do not linger unnecessarily in homes or group residences where their current and long-term essential physical, psychological, and emotional health are at risk.

Traditional adoption of young infants with no history of significant early adversity is declining in most countries, and even where it still exists, the number of infant placements remains relatively low compared to the past. Intercountry adoptions are also declining. Meanwhile, other forms of adoption remain quite prevalent or are on the rise (e.g., foster care adoptions; open adoptions; adoptions by sexual minority adults) and offer the promise of legal, residential, and relational permanence for children in need (Palacios, Adroher, et al., 2019). Adoption is an important turning point that changes the life of adopted persons and their families. Research provides the knowledge base to ensure that the way adoption is practiced at the levels of policy, professional intervention, and family life responds to the complex needs of all those involved to ensure them a healthy, positive personal and social adjustment and development.

Adoption policy and practice must respect international treaties, domestic legislation, and other legal and ethical standards and rules to ensure that they are conducted within a strict rights and ethics framework. Adoption should only become children's permanency plan if it serves their immediate and long-term interests and is lawfully decided on a case-by-case basis, as discussed in Palacios, Adroher, et al. (2019). Adoption is rightly criticized when it is not child-centered and when any malpractice in decision-making or procedures is involved. But if it respects all international and national rules and guarantees, adoption may be one of the best alternatives for children who need a family for life.

References

Almas, A. N., Degnan, K. A., Nelson, C. A., Zeanah, C. H., & Fox, N. A. (2016). IQ at age 12 following a history of institutional care: Findings from the Bucharest Early Intervention Project. *Developmental Psychology, 52*(11), 1858–1866. https://doi.org/10.1037/dev0000167.

American Academy of Pediatrics Council on Foster Care, Adoption, and Kinship Care; Waite, D., Greiner, M. V., & Laris, Z. (2018). Putting families first: How the opioid epidemic is affecting children and families, and the child welfare policy options to address it. *Journal of Applied Research on Children: Informing Policy for Children at Risk, 9*(1), 4, https://doi.org/10.58464/2155-5834.1353.

Anderman, E. M., Ha, S. Y., & Liu, X. (2022). Academic achievement and postsecondary educational attainment of domestically and internationally adopted youth. *Adoption Quarterly, 25*(4), 326–350. https://doi.org/10.1080/10926755.2021.1978025.

Anthony, R. E., Paine, A. L., & Shelton, K. H. (2019). Adverse childhood experiences of children adopted from care: The importance of adoptive parental warmth for future child adjustment. *International Journal of Environmental Research and Public Health, 16*(12), 2212. https://doi.org/10.3390/ijerph16122212.

Aramburu, I., Perez-Testor, C., Mercadal, J. et al. (2020). Influence of communicative openness on the psychological adjustment of internationally adopted adolescents. *Journal of Research on Adolescence, 30*(S1), 226–237. https://doi.org/10.1111/jora.12464.

Askeland, K. G., Hysing, M., La Greca, A. M. et al. (2017). Mental health in internationally adopted adolescents: A meta-analysis. *Journal of the American Academy of Child & Adolescent Psychiatry, 56*(3), 203–213. https://doi.org/10.1016/j.jaac.2016.12.009.

Atkinson, A. J. (2020). Adoption competent clinical practice. In G. M. Wrobel, E. Helder, & E. Marr (Eds.), *The Routledge Handbook of Adoption* (pp. 435–448). Routledge.

Atkinson, A. J. & Gonet, P. (2007). Strengthening adoption practice, listening to adoptive families. *Child Welfare, 86*(2), 87–104.

Audet, K. & Le Mare, L. (2011). Mitigating effects of the adoptive caregiving environment on inattention/overactivity in children adopted from Romanian orphanages. *International Journal of European Development, 35*(2), 107–115. https://doi.org/10.1177/0165025410373313.

Baden, A. (2016). "Do you know your real parents?" and other adoption microaggressions. *Adoption Quarterly, 19*(1), 1–25. https://doi.org/10.1080/10926755.2015.1026012.

Bakermans-Kranenburg, M. J. & van IJzendoorn, M. H. (2015). The hidden efficacy of interventions: Gene×Environment experiments from a differential susceptibility perspective. *Annual Review of Psychology, 66*, 381–409. https://doi.org/10.1146/annurev-psych-010814-015407.

Baran, A. & Pannor, R. (1990). Open adoption. In D. M. Brodzinsky & M. D. Schechter (Eds.), *The Psychology of Adoption* (pp. 316–331). Oxford University Press.

Baran, A. & Pannor, R. (1993). Perspectives on open adoption. *The Future of Children, 11*(1), 119–124. https://doi.org/10.2307/1602406.

Barth, R. P. & Berry, M. (1990). Preventing adoption disruption. *Prevention in Human Services, 9*, 205–222. https://psycnet.apa.org/doi/10.1300/J293v09n01_13.

Battalen, A. W., Dow-Fleisner, S., Brodzinsky, D., & McRoy, R. (2019). Lesbian, gay, and heterosexual adoptive parents' attitudes towards racial socialization practices. *Journal of Evidence-Based Social Work, 16*(2), *178–191.* https://psycnet.apa.org/doi/10.1080/23761407.2019.1576565.

Beesley, P. (2020). *Making Good Assessments*. CoramBAAF.

Behle, A. E. & Pinquart, M. (2016). Psychiatric disorders and treatment in adoptees: A meta-analytic comparison with non-adoptees. *Adoption Quarterly, 19*(4), 284–306. https://doi.org/10.1080/10926755.2016.1201708.

Belsky, J. & van IJzendoorn, M. H. (2017). Genetic differential susceptibility to the effects of parenting. *Current Opinion in Psychology, 15*, 125–130. https://doi.org/10.1016/j.copsyc.2017.02.021.

Bornstein, M. H. (1989). Sensitive periods in development: Structural characteristics and causal interpretations. *Psychological Bulletin, 105*(2), 179–197. https://doi.org/10.1037/0033-2909.105.2.179.

Bornstein, M. H. & Suwalsky, J. T. D. (2021). The specificity principle in adoption. *Journal of Applied Developmental Psychology, 74*, 101264. https://doi.org/10.1016/j.appdev.2021.101264.

Bos, H. & Gartrell, N. (2020). Lesbian-mother families formed through donor insemination. In. A. E. Goldberg & K. R. Allen (Eds.), *LGBTQ Parent Families: Innovations in Research and Implications for Practice* (pp. 25–44) (2nd ed.). Springer.

Bowes, L. & Jaffee, S. R. (2013). Biology, genes, and resilience: Toward a multidisciplinary approach. *Trauma, Violence, & Abuse, 14*(3), 195–208. https://doi.org/10.1177/1524838013487807.

Bowie, F. (2004) (Ed.). *Cross Cultural Approaches to Adoption*. Routledge.

Boyle, C. (2017). "What is the impact of birth family contact on children in adoption and long-term foster care?" A systematic review. *Child and Family Social Work, 22*(S1), 22–33. https://doi.org/10.1111/cfs.12236.

Brett, Z. H., Humphreys, K. L., Smyke, A. T. et al. (2015). Serotonin transporter linked polymorphic region (5-HTTLPR) genotype moderates the longitudinal impact of early caregiving on externalizing behavior. *Development and Psychopathology, 27*(1), 7–18. https://doi.org/10.1017/S0954579414001266.

Brodzinsky, D. M. (1990). A stress and coping model of adoption adjustment. In D. M. Brodzinsky & M. D. Schechter (Eds.), *The Psychology of Adoption* (pp. 3–24). Oxford University Press.

Brodzinsky, D. M. (2005). Reconceptualizing openness in adoption: Implications for theory, research, and practice. In D. M. Brodzinsky & J. Palacios (Eds.), *Psychological Issues in Adoption: Research and Practice* (pp.145–166). Praeger.

Brodzinsky, D. M. (2006). Family structural openness and communication openness as predictors in the adjustment of adopted children. *Adoption Quarterly, 9*(4), 1–18. https://doi.org/10.1300/J145v09n04_01.

Brodzinsky, D. M. (2008). *Adoptive Parent Preparation Project Phase 1: Meeting the Mental Health and Developmental Needs of Adopted Children*. Donaldson Adoption Institute. www.nationalcenteronadoptionandperma nency.net/post/adoptive-parent-preparation-project-phase-i.

Brodzinsky, D. M. (2011a). *Expanding Resources for Children III: Research-Based Best Practices in Adoption by Gays and Lesbians*. Donaldson Adoption Institute. www.nationalcenteronadoptionandpermanency.net/post/ research-based-best-practices-in-adoption-by-gays-and-lesbians.

Brodzinsky, D. M. (2011b). Children's understanding of adoption: Developmental and clinical implications. *Professional Psychology: Research and Practice, 42* (2), 200–207. https://doi/10.1037/a0022415.

Brodzinsky, D. M. (2012). Adoption by lesbians and gay men: A national survey of adoption agency policies and practices. In D. M. Brodzinsky & A. Pertman (Eds.), *Adoption by Lesbians and Gay Men: A New Dimension in Family Diversity* (pp. 62–84). Oxford University Press.

Brodzinsky, D. M. (2013). *A Need to Know: Enhancing Adoption Competence among Mental Health Professionals*. Donald Adoption Institute. www.natio nalcenteronadoptionandpermanency.net/post/a-need-to-know-enhancing-adoption-competence-amongmental-health-professionals-policy-perspective.

Brodzinsky, D. (2014). The role of birthparents in the life of the adoptive family: Real versus symbolic presence. In E. Scabini & G. Rossi (Eds.),

Allargare lo spazio familiare: Adozione e affido. Studi interdisciplinary sulla famiglia. N. 27 (pp. 223–238). Milan: vita e Pensiero.

Brodzinsky, D. M. (In press). International adoption. In A. Goldberg (Ed.), *Encyclopedia of LGBTQ Studies* (2nd ed.). Sage.

Brodzinsky, D. M. & Goldberg, A. E. (2016). Contact with birth families in adoptive families headed by lesbian, gay male, and heterosexual parents. *Children and Youth Services Review, 62,* 9–17. https://doi.org/10.1016/j .childyouth.2016.01.014.

Brodzinsky, D. & Goldberg, A. (2017). Contact with birth family in intercountry adoptions: Comparing families headed by sexual minority and heterosexual parents. *Children and Youth Services Review, 74,* 117–124. https://doi .org/10.1016/j.childyouth.2017.02.003.

Brodzinsky, D., Gunnar, M., & Palacios, J. (2022). Adoption and trauma: Risks, recovery, and the lived experience of adoption. *Child Abuse & Neglect, 130* (Pt 2), 105309. https://doi.org/10.1016/j.chiabu.2021.105309.

Brodzinsky, D., Santa, J., & Smith, S. L. (2016). Adopted youth in residential care: Prevalence rate and professional training needs. *Residential Treatment for Children & Youth, 33*(2), 118–134. https://doi.org/10.1080/ 0886571X.2016.1175993.

Brodzinsky, D. M., Schechter, M. D., & Henig, R. M. (1992). *Being Adopted: The Lifelong Search for Self.* Doubleday.

Brodzinsky, D. M., Singer, L., & Braff, A. M. (1984). Children's understanding of adoption. *Child Development, 55*(3), 869–878. https://doi.org/10.2307/ 1130138.

Brown, A., Waters, C. S., & Shelton, K. H. (2017). A systematic review of the school performance and behavioural and emotional adjustments of children adopted from care. *Adoption & Fostering, 41*(4), 346–368. https://doi.org/ 10.1177/0308575917731064.

Cadoret, R. J., Yates, W. R., Troughton, E., Woodworth, G., & Stewart, M. A. (1995). Adoption study demonstrating two genetic pathways to drug abuse. *Archives of General Psychiatry, 52,* 42–52. https://doi.org/10.1001/ archpsyc.1995.03950130042005.

Canzi, E., Rosnati, R., Palacios, J., & Román, M. (2017). Internationally adopted children's cognitive and social-emotional development during the first postadoption year: A longitudinal study. *European Journal of Developmental Psychology, 15*(4), 517–530. https://doi:10.1080/17405629.2017.1316257.

Carlson, E., Hostinar, C., Mliner, S., & Gunnar, M. (2014). The emergence of attachment following early social deprivation. *Development and Psychopathology, 26*(2), 479–489. https://doi.org./10.1017/S095457 9414000078.

Cheeseman, R., Hunjan, A., Coleman, J. R. I. et al. (2020). Comparison of adopted and nonadopted individuals reveals gene-environment interplay for education in the UK Biobank. *Psychological Science, 31*(5), 582–591. https://doi.org/10.1177/0956797620904450.

Colaner, C. W. (2014). Measuring adoptive identity: Validation of the adoptive identity work scale. *Adoption Quarterly, 17*(2), 134–157. https://doi.org/10.1080/10926755.2014.891546.

Colaner, C. W. & Soliz, J. (2015). A communicated-based approach to adoptive identity: Theoretical and empirical support. *Communication Research, 44*(5), 611–637. https://doi.org/10.1177/0093650215577860.

Colaner, C. W., Horstman, H. K., & Rittenour, C. E. (2018). Negotiating adoptive and birth shared family identity: A social identity complexity approach. *Western Journal of Communication, 82*(4), 393–415. https://doi.org/10.1080/10570314.2017.1384564.

Colich, N. L., Sheridan, M. A., Humphreys, K. L. et al. (2021). Heightened sensitivity to the caregiving environment during adolescence: Implications for recovery following early-life adversity. *Journal of Child Psychology and Psychiatry, and Allied Disciplines, 62*(8), 937–940. https://doi.org/10.1111/jcpp.13347.

Colonnesi, C., Wissink, I. B., Noom, M. J. et al. (2013). Basic trust: An attachment-oriented intervention based on mind-mindedness in adoptive families. *Research in Social Work Practice, 23*(2), 179–188. https://doi.org/10.1177/1049731512469301.

Colonnesi, C., Zeegers, M. A. J., Majdandzic, M., van Steensel, F. J. A., & Bögels, S. M. (2019). Fathers' and mothers' early mind-mindedness predicts social competence and behavior problems in childhood. *Journal of Abnormal Child Psychology, 47*, 1421–1435. https://doi.org/10.1007/s10802-019-00537-2.

Cree, R. A., Liu, C., Gueorguieva, R. et al. (2021). Using an adoption design to test genetically based differences in risk for child behavior problems in response to home environmental influences. *Development and Psychopathology, 33*(4), 1229–1247. https://doi.org/10.1017/S0954579420000450.

Dalen, M. (2005). International adoptions in Scandinavia: Research focus and main results. In D. M. Brodzinsky & J. Palacios (Eds.), *Psychological Issues in Adoption: Research and Practice* (pp. 211–231). Praeger.

Dhami, M. K., Mandel, D. R., & Sothmann, K. (2007). An evaluation of postadoption services. *Children and Youth Services Review, 29*, 162–179. https://psycnet.apa.org/doi/10.1016/j.childyouth.2006.06.03.

Doka, K. J, (1989). Disenfranchised grief. In K. J. Doka (Ed.), *Disenfranchised Grief: Recognizing Hidden Sorrow* (pp. 3–11). Lexington Books.

Dozier, M. & Rutter, M. (2016). Challenges to the development of attachment relationships faced by young children in foster and adoptive care. In J. Cassidy & P. R. Shaver (Eds.), *Handbook of Attachment: Theory, Research, and Clinical Applications* (pp. 696–714). Guilford Press.

Dunbar, N. & Grotevant, H. D. (2004). Adoption narratives: The construction of adoptive identity during adolescence. In M. W. Pratt & B. H. Fiese (Eds.), *Family Stories and the Life Course: Across Time and Generations* (pp. 135–161). Lawrence Erlbaum.

Duncan, M., Woolgar, M., Ransley, R., & Fearson, P. (2021). Mental health and behavioral difficulties in adopted children: A systematic review of postadoption risk and protective factors. *Adoption and Fostering, 45*(4), 414–429. https://doi.org/10.1177/03085759211058358.

Éthier, L. S., Lemelin, J. P., & Lacharité, C. (2004). A longitudinal study of the effects of chronic maltreatment on children's behavioral and emotional problems. *Child Abuse & Neglect, 28*(12), 1265–1278. https://doi.org/10.1016/j.chiabu.2004.07.006.

Farr, R. H. (2017). Does parental sexual orientation matter? A longitudinal follow-up of adoptive families with school-age children. *Developmental Psychology, 53*(2), 252–264. https://psycnet.apa.org/doi/10.1037/dev0000228.

Farr, R. H., Grant-Marsney, H. A., & Grotevant, H. D. (2014). Adoptees' contact with birth parents in emerging adulthood: The role of adoption communication and attachment to adoptive parents. *Family Process, 53*(4), 656–671. https://doi.org/10.1111/famp.12069.

Farr, R. H., Ravvina, Y., & Grotevant, H. D. (2018). Birth family contact experiences among lesbian, gay, and heterosexual adoptive parents with school-age children. *Family Relations: Interdisciplinary Journal of Applied Family Science, 67*(1), 132–146. https://doi.org/10.1111/fare.12295.

Farr, R. H., Vasquez, C. P., & Lapidus, E. P. (2022). Birth relatives' perspectives about same-gender parent adoptive family placements. *Family Process, 62* (2), 624–640 . https://doi.org/10.1111/famp.12795.

Farr, R. H., Vasquez, C. P., & Patterson, C. J. (2020). LGBTQ adoptive parents and their children. In A. E. Goldberg & K. R. Allen (Eds.), *LGBTQ Parent Families: Innovations in Research and Implications for Practice* (pp. 45–64) (2nd ed.). Springer.

Ferrari, L. & Rosnati, R. (2022). Intercountry adoption migration process: Cultural challenges and resources to promote psychosocial well-being. In M. Fatigante, C. Zucchermaglio, & F. Alby (Eds.), *Interculturality in Institutions: Culture in Policy Making* (pp. 249–263). Springer, Cham. https://doi.org/10.1007/978-3-031-12626-0_12.

Ferrari, L., Caravita, S., Ranieri, S., Canzi, E., & Rosnati, R. (2022). Bullying victimization among internationally adopted adolescents: Psychosocial adjustment and moderating factors. *Plos One, 17*(2), e0262726.

Ferrari, L., Rosnati, R., Manzi, C., & Benet-Martinez, V. (2015). Ethnic identity, bicultural identity integration, and psychological well-being among transracial adoptees: A longitudinal study. *New Directions for Child & Adolescent Development, 2015*(150), 63–76. https://doi.org/10.1002/cad.20122.

Finet, C., Vermeer, H. J., Juffer, F., & Bosmans, G. (2018). Behavioral adjustment of Chinese adoptees: The role of preadoption experiences. *Children and Youth Services Review, 86*, 226–235. https://doi.org/10.1016/j.childyouth.2018.01.029.

Foli, K. J, South, S. C., & Lim, E. (2012). Rates and predictors of depression in adoptive mothers: Moving toward a theory. *Advances in Nursing Science, 35*(1), 51–63. https://doi.org/10.1097/ANS.0b013e318244553e.

Fonagy, P., Campbell, C., & Luyten, P. (2023). Attachment, mentalizing and trauma: Then (1992) and now (2022). *Brain Sciences, 13*(3), 459. https://doi.org/10.3390/brainsci13030459.

Fox, N. A., Almas, A. N., Degnan, K. A., Nelson, C. A., & Zeanah, C. H. (2011). The effects of severe psychosocial deprivation and foster care intervention on cognitive development at 8 years of age: Findings from the Bucharest Early Intervention Project. *Journal of Child Psychology and Psychiatry, and Allied Disciplines, 52*(9), 919–928. https://doi.org/10.1111/J.1469-7610.2010.02355.x.

French, Q. Y. S. (2013). Adoption as a contingency of self-worth: An integrative approach to self-esteem in adopted individuals. *Adoption Quarterly, 16*(2), 128–152. https://doi.org/10.1080/10926755.2013.787574.

French, V. (2019). Ancient history of parenting. In M. H. Bornstein (Ed.), *Biology and Ecology of Parenting: Handbook of Parenting* (3rd ed., Vol. 2, pp. 287–319). Routledge.

Gagnon-Oosterwaal, N., Cossette, L., Smolla, N. et al. (2012). Preadoption adversity, maternal stress, and behavior problems at school-age in international adoptees. *Journal of Applied Developmental Psychology, 33*(5), 236–242. https://doi.org/10.1016/j.appdev.2012.04.002.

Garber, K. J. & Grotevant, H. D. (2015). "You were adopted?!": Microaggressions toward adolescent adopted individuals in same-race families. *The Counseling Psychologist, 43*(3), 435–462. https://doi.org/10.1177/0011000014566471.

Gates, G. (2013). *LGBTQ Parenting in the United States.* Technical Report. The Williams Institute.

Ge, X., Natsuaki, M. N., Martin, D. M. et al. (2008). Bridging the divide: Openness in adoption and postadoption psychological adjustment among birth and adoptive parents. *Journal of Family Psychology, 22*(4), 529–540. https://psycnet.apa.org/doi/10.1037/a0012817.

Goldberg, A. E. (2019). *Open Adoption and Diverse Families: Complex Relationships in the Digital Age.* Oxford University Press.

Goldberg, A. E. & Garcia, R. L. (2016). Gender-typed behavior over time in children with lesbian, gay, and heterosexual parents. *Journal of Family Psychology, 30*(7), 854–865. https://psycnet.apa.org/doi/10.1037/fam0000226.

Goldberg, A. E., Frost, R. I., Miranda, I., & Kahn, E. (2019). LGBTQ individuals' experiences with delays and disruptions in the foster and adoption process. *Children and Youth Services Review, 106,* 104466. https://doi.org/10.1016/j.childyouth.2019.104466.

Goldberg, A. E. & Smith, J. (2009). Predicting non-African American lesbian and heterosexual preadoptive couples' openness to adopting an African American child. *Family Relations, 58*(3), 346–360. https://doi.org/10.1111/j.1741-3729.2009.00557.x.

Goldberg, A. E. & Smith, J. (2013). Predictors of psychological adjustment in early placed adopted children with lesbian, gay, and heterosexual parents. *Journal of Family Psychology, 27*(3), 431–442. https://psycnet.apa.org/doi/10.1037/a0032911.

Golombok, S. (2015). *Modern Families: Parents and Children in New Family Forms.* Cambridge University Press.

Golombok, S., Mellish, L., Jennings, S. et al. (2014). Adoptive gay father families: Parent-child relationships and children's psychological adjustment. *Child Development, 85*(2), 456–468. https://doi.org/10.1111/cdev.12155.

Grotevant, H. D. (2009). Emotional distance regulation over the life course in adoptive kinship networks. In G. M. Wrobel & E. Neil (Eds.), *International Advances in AdoptionResearch for Practice* (pp. 295–316). Wiley-Blackwell.

Grotevant, H. D. (2020). Open adoption. In G. M. Wrobel & E. Helder (Eds.), *The Routledge Handbook of Adoption* (pp. 266–277). Routledge.

Grotevant, H. D., Dunbar, N., Kohler, J. K., & Esau, A. (2000). Adoptive identity: How contexts within and beyond the family shape developmental pathways. *Family Relations, 49*(4), 379–387. https://doi.org/10.1111/j.1741-3729.2000.00379.x.

Grotevant, H. D., Lo, A. Y. H., Fiorenzo, L., & Dunbar, N. D. (2017). Adoptive identity and adjustment from adolescence to emerging adulthood: A person-centered approach. *Developmental Psychology, 53*(11), 2195–2204. https://psycnet.apa.org/doi/10.1037/dev0000352.

Grotevant, H. D., McRoy, R. G., Elde, C., & Fravel, D. L. (1994). Adoptive family system dynamics: Variations by level of openness in the adoption. *Family Process, 33*(2), 125–146. https://doi.org/10.1111/j.1545-5300.1994.00125.x.

Grotevant, H. D., Rueter, M., Von Korff, L., & Gonzalez, D. (2011). Postadoption contact, adoption communication openness, and satisfaction with contact as predictors of externalizing behavior in adolescence and emerging adulthood. *Journal of Child Psychology and Psychiatry, 52*(5), 529–536. https://doi.org/10.1111/j.1469-7610.2010.02330.x.

Grotevant, H. D. & von Korff, L. (2011). Adoptive identity. In S. J. Schwartz, K. Luyckx, & V. L. Vignoles (Eds.), *Handbook of Identity Theory and Research* (pp. 585–601). Springer.

Grotevant, H. D., Wrobel, G. M., Fiorenzo, L., Lo, A. Y., & McRoy, R. G. (2019). Trajectories of birth family contact in domestic adoptions. *Journal of Family Psychology, 33*(1), 54–63. https://psycnet.apa.org/doi/10.1037/fam0000449.

Gunnar, M. R., DePasquale, C. E., Reid, B. M., Donzella, B., & Miller, B. S. (2019). Pubertal stress recalibration reverses the effects of early life stress in postinstitutionalized children. *Proceedings of the National Academy of Sciences, 116*(48),23984–23988. https://doi.org/10.1073/pnas.1909699116.

Gunnar, M. R. & Reid, B. M. (2019). Early deprivation revisited: Contemporary studies of the impact on young children institutional care. In S. Gelman & S. Waxman (Eds.), *Annual Review of Developmental Psychology* (Vol. 1, pp. 93–118). https://doi.org/10.1146/annurev-devpsych1213-085013.

Hails, K. A., Shaw, D. S., Leve, L. D. et al. (2018). Interaction between adoptive mothers' and fathers' depressive symptoms in risk for children's emerging problem behavior. *Social Development, 28*(3), 725–742. https://doi.org/10.1111/sode.12352.

Hartinger-Saunders, R. M., Trouteaud, A., & Johnson, J. M. (2015). Post adoption services needs and use as predictors of adoption dissolution: Findings from the 2012 national adoptive families study. *Adoption Quarterly, 18*(4), 255–272. https://doi.org/10.1080/10926755.2014.895469.

Haugaard J. J. (1998). Is adoption a risk factor for the development of adjustment problems? *Clinical Psychology Review, 18*(1), 47–69. https://doi.org/10.1016/s0272-7358(97)00055-x.

Hawkins, A., Beckett, C., Rutter, M. et al. (2007). Communicative openness about adoption and interest in a sample of domestic and intercountry adolescent adoptees. *Adoption Quarterly, 10*(3–4), 131–156. https://doi.org/10.1080/10926750802163220.

Helder, E. J., Mulder, E., & Gunnoe, M. L. (2016). A longitudinal investigation of children internationally adopted at school age. *Child Neuropsychology, 22* (1), 39–64. https://doi.org/10.1080/09297049.2014.967669.

Hindle, D. & Shulman, G. (Eds.) (2008). *The Emotional Experience of Adoption: A Psychanalytic Perspective*. Routledge.

Hjern, A., Vinnerljung, B., & Brännström, L. (2019). Outcomes in adulthood of adoption after long-term foster care: A sibling study. *Developmental Child Welfare, 1*(1), 61–75. https://doi.org/10.1177/2516103218815702.

Hornfeck, F., Bovenschen, I., Heene, S. et al. (2019). Emotional and behavior problems in adopted children. The role of early adversities and adoptive parents' regulation and behavior. *Child Abuse & Neglect, 98*, 104221. https://doi.org/10.1016/j.chiabu.2019.104221.

Horstmann, H. K., Colaner, C. W., & Rittenour, C. E. (2016). Contributing factors of adult adoptees' identity work and self-esteem: Family communication patterns and adoption-specific communication. *Journal of Family Communication, 16*, 263–276. https://doi.org/10.1080/15267431.2016.1181069.

Hostinar, C. E., Stellern, S. A., Schaefer, C., Carlson, S. M., & Gunnar, M. R. (2012). Associations between early life adversity and executive function in children adopted internationally from orphanages. *Proceedings of the National Academy of Sciences of the United States of America, 109* (Suppl 2), 17208–17212. https://doi.org/10.1073/pnas.1121246109.

Howard, J. A., Smith, S., & Ryan, S. D. (2004). A comparative study of child welfare adoptions with other types of adopted children and birth children. *Adoption Quarterly, 7*(3), 1–30. https://doi.org/10.1300/J145v07n03_01.

Hrapczynski, K. M. & Leslie, L. A. (2018). Engagement in racial socialization among transracial adoptive families with White parents. *Family Relations, 67* (3), 354–367. https://doi.org/10.1111/fare.12316.

Hu, A. W., Anderson, K. N., & Lee, R. M. (2015). Let's talk about race and ethnicity: Cultural socialization, parenting quality, and ethnic identity development. *Family Science, 6*(1), 87–93. https://doi.org/10.1080/19424620.2015 .1081007.

Ivey, R., Kerac, M., Quiring, M. et al. (2021). The nutritional status of individuals adopted internationally as children: A systematic review. *Nutrients, 13* (1), 245. https://doi.org/10.3390/nu13010245.

Johnson, D. E. & Gunnar, M. R. (2011). Growth failure in institutionalized children. *Monographs of the Society for Research on Child Development, 76*, 92–126. https://doi.org/10.1111/j.1540-5834.2011.00629.x.

Johnson, D. E., Tang, A., Almas, A. N. et al. (2018). Caregiving disruptions affect growth and pubertal development in early adolescence in institutionalized and fostered Romanian children: A randomized clinical trial. *The Journal of Pediatrics*, *203*, 345–353.e3. https://doi.org/10.1016/j.jpeds.2018.07.027.

Johnston, K. E., Swim, J. K., Saltsman, B. M., Deater-Deckard, K., & Petrill, S. A. (2007). Mothers' racial, ethnic, and cultural socialization of transracially adopted Asian children. *Family Relations*, *56*(4), 390–402. https://doi.org/10.1111/j.1741-3729.2007.00468.x.

Juffer, F. & van IJzendoorn, M. H. (2005). Behavior problems and mental health referrals of international adoptees: A meta-analysis. *JAMA*, *293*(20), 2501–2515. https://doi.org/10.1001/jama.293.20.2501.

Juffer, F. & van IJzendoorn, M. H. (2007). Adoptees do not lack self-esteem: A meta-analysis of studies on self-esteem of transracial, international, and domestic adoptees. *Psychological Bulletin*, *133*(6), 1067–1083. https://doi/10.1037/0033-2909.133.6.1067.

Juffer, F., Bakermans-Kranenburg, M. J., & van IJzendoorn, M. H. (Eds.) (2008). *Promoting Positive Parenting: An Attachment-Based Intervention*. Taylor & Francis.

Kendler, K. S., Morris, N. A., Ohlsson, H. et al. (2016). Criminal offending and the family environment: Swedish national high-risk home-reared and adopted-away co-sibling control study. *The British Journal of Psychiatry*, *209*(4), 294–299. https://doi.org/10.1192/bjp.bp.114.159558.

Kendler, K. S., Ohlsson, H., Sundquist, J., & Sundquist, K. (2020). The rearing environment and risk for major depression: A Swedish national high-risk home-reared and adopted-away co-sibling control study. *The American Journal of Psychiatry*, *177*(5), 447–453. https://doi.org/10.1176/appi.ajp.2019.19090911.

Kendler, K. S., Ohlsson, H., Sundquist, J., & Sundquist, K. (2021). The rearing environment and the risk for alcohol use disorder: A Swedish national high-risk home-reared *v.* adopted co-sibling control study. *Psychological Medicine*, *51*(14), 2370–2377. https://doi.org/10.1017/S0033291720000963.

Kendler, K. S., Turkheimer, E., Ohlsson, H., Sundquist, J., & Sundquist, K. (2015). Family environment and the malleability of cognitive ability: A Swedish national home-reared and adopted-away cosibling control study. *Proceedings of the National Academy of Sciences of the United States of America*, *112*(15), 4612–4617. https://doi.org/10.1073/pnas.1417106112.

Killian, C. & Khana, N. (2019). Beyond color-blind and color-conscious: Approaches to racial socialization among parents of transracially adopted children. *Family Relations*, *68*(2), 260–274. https://doi.org/10.1111/fare.12357.

Kirk, H. D. (1964). *Shared Fate: A Theory and Method of Adoptive Relationships*. Free Press.

Kohler, J. K., Grotevant, H. D., & McRoy, R. G. (2002). Adopted adolescents' preoccupation with adoption: The impact on adoptive family relationships. *Journal of Marriage and Family, 64*(1), 93–104. https://doi.org/10.1111/j.1741-3737.2002.00093.x.

Koren, G. & Ornoy, A. (2020). Searching for the fetal alcohol behavioral phenotype. *Global Pediatric Health, 7*, 1–6. https://doi.org/2333794X20941337.

Koskinen, M. G. & Böök, M. L. (2019). Searching for the self: Adult international adoptees' narratives of their search for and reunion with their birth families. *Adoption Quarterly, 22*(3), 219–246. https://doi.org/10.1080/10926755.2019.1627449.

Kraft, A., Palumbo, J., Woods, P., Schmidt, A., & Tucker, N. (1985). Some theoretical considerations on confidential adoptions. Part 3: The adopted child. *Child and Adolescent Social Work, 2*, 139–153. https://doi.org/10.1007/BF00758065.

Kriebel, D. K. & Wentzel, K. (2011). Parenting as a moderator of cumulative risk for behavior competence in adopted children. *Adoption Quarterly, 14*(1), 37–60. https://doi.org/10.1080/10926755.2011.557945.

Kroupina, M. G., Eckerle, J. K., Fuglestad, A. J. et al. (2015). Associations between physical growth and general cognitive functioning in international adoptees from Eastern Europe at 30 months post-arrival. *Journal of Neurodevelopmental Disorders, 7*(1), 1–9. https://doi.org/10.1186/s11689-015-9132-7.

Lawler, J. M., Koss, K. J., & Gunnar, M. R. (2017). Bidirectional effects of parenting and child behavior in internationally adopting families. *Journal of Family Psychology, 31*(5), 563–573. https://psycnet.apa.org/doi/10.1037/fam0000309.

Lee, R. M. (2003). The transracial paradox: History, research, and counseling implications of cultural socialization. *The Counseling Psychologist, 31*(6), 711–744. https://doi.org/10.1177/0011000003258087.

Lee, B. R., Battalen, A. W., Brodzinsky, D. B., & Goldberg, A. E. (2020). Parent, child, and adoption characteristics associated with postadoption support needs. *Social Work Research, 44*(1), 21–32. https://doi.org/10.1093/swr/svz026.

Lee, B. R., Kobulsky, J. M., Brodzinsky, D. M., & Barth, R. P. (2018). Parent perspectives on adoption preparation: Findings from the modern adoptive families project. *Children and Youth Services Review, 85*, 63–71. https://doi.org/10.1016/j.childyouth.2017.12.007.

Lee, R. M., Grotevant, H. D., Hellerstedt, W. L., Gunnar, M.R., & Minnesota International Adoption Project Team (2006). Cultural socialization in families with internationally adopted children. *Journal of Family Psychology, 20*(4), 571–580. https://psycnet.apa.org/doi/10.1037/0893-3200.20.4.571.

Le Mare, L., & Audet, K. (2011). Communicative openness in adoption: Knowledge of culture of origin, and adoption identity in adolescents adopted from Romania. *Adoption Quarterly, 14*(3), 199–217. https://doi.org/10.1080/10926755.2011.608031.

Leroy, J. L., Frongillo, E. A., Dewan, P., Black, M. M., & Waterland, R. A. (2020). Can children catch up from the consequences of undernourishment? Evidence from child linear growth, developmental epigenetics, and brain and neurocognitive development. *Advances in Nutrition, 11*(4), 1032–1041. https://doi.org/10.1093/advances/nmaa020.

Leve, L. D., Griffin, A. M., Natsuaki, M. N. et al. (2019). Longitudinal examination of pathways to peer problems in middle childhood: A siblings-reared-apart design. *Development and Psychopathology, 31*(5), 1633–1647. https://doi:10.1017/S0954579419000890.

Liskola, K., Raaska, H., Lapinleimu, H., & Elovainio, M. (2018). Parental depressive symptoms as a risk factor for child depressive symptoms: Testing the social mediators in internationally adopted children. *European Child & Adolescent Psychiatry, 27*(12), 1585–1593. https://doi.org/10.1007/s00787-018-1154-8.

Lionetti, F. (2014). What promotes secure attachment in early adoption? The protective roles of infants' temperament and adoptive parents' attachment. *Attachment and Human Development, 16*(6), 573–589. https://doi.org/10.1080/14616734.2014.959028.

Lionetti, F., Pastore, M., & Barone, L. (2015). Attachment in institutionalized children: A review and meta-analysis. *Child Abuse & Neglect, 42*, 135–145. https://doi.org/10.1016/j.chiabu.2015.02.013.

Lo, A. Y. H. & Cashen, K. K. (2020). How adoptive parents think about their role as parents. In G. M. Wrobel, E. Helder, & E. Marr (Eds.), *The Routledge Handbook of Adoption* (pp. 278–290). Routledge.

Lo, A. Y. H. & Grotevant, H. D. (2020). Adoptive parenting cognitions: Acknowledgment of differences as a predictor of adolescents' attachment to parents. *Parenting: Science and Practice, 20*(2), 83–107. https://doi.org/10.1080/15295192.2019.1694826.

Lo, A. Y. H., Grotevant, H. D., & Wrobel, G. M. (2023). Birth family contact from childhood to adulthood: Adjustment and adoption outcomes in adopted young adults. *International Journal of Behavioral Development*, online publication April 1. https://doi.org/10.1177/01650254231165839.

Mackes, N., Golm, D., Sarkar, S. et al. (2020). Early childhood deprivation is associated with alterations in adult brain structure despite subsequent environmental enrichment. *Proceedings of the National Academy of Sciences, 117*(1), 641–649. https://doi.org/10.1073/pnas.1911264116.

Manzi, C., Ferrari, L., Rosnati, R., & Benet-Martinez, V. (2014). Bicultural identity integration of transracial adolescent adoptees: Antecedents and outcomes. *Journal of Cross-Cultural Psychology*, *45*(6), 888–904. https://doi.org/10.1177/0022022114530495.

Mason, P. W., Johnson, D. E., & Prock, L. A. (2014). *Adoption Medicine: Caring for Children and Families*. American Academy of Pediatrics.

Masten, A. S. (2011). Resilience in children threatened by extreme adversity: Frameworks for research, practice, and translational synergy. *Development and Psychopathology*, *23*(2), 493–506. https://doi.org/10.1017/S0954579411000198.

McConnachie, A. L., Ayed, N., Foley, S. et al. (2021). Adoptive gay father families: A longitudinal study of children's adjustment at early adolescence. *Child Development*, *92*(1), 425–443. https://doi.org/10.1111/cdev.13442.

McLaughlin, K. A., Zeanah, C. H., Fox, N. A., & Nelson, C. A. (2012). Attachment security as a mechanism linking foster care placement to improved mental health outcomes in previously institutionalized children. *Journal of Child Psychology and Psychiatry*, *53*(1), 46–55. https://doi.org/10.1111/j.1469-7610.2011.02437.x.

Meakings, S., Paine, A. L., & Shelton, K. H. (2021). Birth sibling relationships after adoption: Experience of contact with brothers and sisters living elsewhere. *British Journal of Social Work*, *51*(7), 2478–2499. https://doi.org/10.1093/bjsw/bcaa053.

Mendenhall, T., Berge, J., Wrobel, G. M., Grotevant, H. D., & McRoy, R. G. (2004). Adolescents' satisfaction with contacts in adoption. *Child and Adolescent Social Work Journal*, *21*(2), 175–190. https://doi.org/10.1023/B:CASW.0000022730.89093.b7.

Merritt, D. H. & Ludeke, R. D. (2020). Postadoption services: Needs and adoption type. In G. M. Wrobel, E. Helder, & E. Marr (Eds.), *The Routledge Handbook of Adoption* (pp. 483–492). Routledge.

Meyer, I. H. (2003). Prejudice, social stress, and mental health in lesbian, gay, and bisexual populations: Conceptual issues and research evidence. *Psychological Bulletin*, *129*(5), 674–697. https://psycnet.apa.org/doi/10.1037/0033-2909.129.5.674.

Mohanty, J. & Newell, C. E. (2011). Asian adolescent and young adult adoptees' psychological well-being: Examining the mediating role of marginality. *Children and Youth Services Review*, *33*(7), 1189–1195. https://doi.org/10.1016/j.childyouth.2011.02.016.

Müller, U. & Perry, B. (2001). Adopted persons' search for and contact with their birth parents: Who searches and why? *Adoption Quarterly*, *4*(3), 5–37. https://doi.org/10.1300/J145v04n03_02.

Murray, K. J., Williams, B. M., Tunno, A. M., Shanahan, M., & Sullivan, K. M. (2022). What about trauma? Accounting for trauma exposure and symptoms in the risk of suicide among adolescents who have been adopted. *Child Abuse & Neglect, 130*(Pt 2), 105185. https://doi.org/10.1016/j.chiabu.2021.105185.

Nadeem, E., Waterman, J., Foster, J. et al. (2017). Long-term effects of pre-placement risk factors on children's psychological symptoms and parenting stress among families adopting children from foster care. *Journal of Emotional and Behavioral Disorders, 25*(2), 67–81. https://doi.org/10.1177/1063426615621050.

Natsuaki, M. N., Stepanyan, S. T., Neiderhiser, J. M. et al. (2021). Do I look gawky? The association between pubertal asynchrony and peer victimization. *Children, 8*, 794. https://doi.org/10.3390/children8090794.

Neil, E., Beek, M., & Ward, E. (2015). *Contact after Adoption: A Longitudinal Study of Post Adoption Contact Arrangements.* CoramBAAF.

Nelson, C. A. & Gabard-Durnam, L. J. (2020). Early adversity and critical periods: Neurodevelopmental consequences of violating the expectable environment. *Trends in Neurosciences, 43*(3), 133–143. https://doi.org/10.1016/j.tins.2020.01.002.

Nelson, C. A., Zeanah, C. H., & Fox, N. A. (2019). How early experience shapes human development: The case of psychosocial deprivation. *Neural Plasticity, 2019*, 1676285. https://doi.org/10.1155/2019/1676285.

Pace, C. S., Di Folco, S., Guerriero, V., & Muzi, S. (2019). Late-adopted children grown up: A long-term longitudinal study on attachment patterns of adolescent adoptees and their adoptive mothers. *Attachment & Human Development, 21*(4), 372–388. https://doi.org/10.1080/14616734.2019.1571519.

Paine, A. L., Fahey, K., Anthony, R. E., & Shelton, K. H. (2021). Early adversity predicts adoptees' enduring emotional and behavioral problems in childhood. *European Child & Adolescent Psychiatry, 30*(5), 721–732. https://doi.org/10.1007/s00787-020-01553-0.

Palacios, J. (2009). The ecology of adoption. In G. M. Wrobel & E. Neil (Eds.), *International advances in adoption research for practice* (pp. 71–94). Wiley-Blackwell.

Palacios, J., Adroher, S., Brodzinsky, D. M. et al. (2019). Adoption in the service of child protection: An international interdisciplinary perspective. *Psychology, Public Policy, and Law, 25*(2), 57–72. https://doi.org/10.1037/law0000192.

Palacios, J. & Brodzinsky, D. (2010). Adoption research: Trends, topics, and outcomes. *International Journal of Behavioral Development, 34*(3), 270–284. https://doi.org/10.1177/0165025410362837.

Palacios, J., Rolock, N., Selwyn, J., & Barbosa-Ducharne, M. (2019). Adoption breakdown: Concept, research, and implications. *Research in Social Work Practice, 29*(2), 130–142. https://doi.org/10.1177/1049731518783852.

Palacios, J., Román, M., & Camacho, C. (2011). Growth and development in internationally adopted children: Extent and timing of recovery after early adversity. *Child: Care, Health and Development, 37*, 282–288. https://doi.org/10.1111/j.1365-2214.2010.01142.x.

Palacios, J., Román, M., Moreno, C., León, E., & Peñarrubia, M. (2014). Differential plasticity in the recovery of adopted children after early adversity. *Child Development Perspectives, 8*(3), 169–174. https://doi.org/10.1111/cdep.12083.

Peñarrubia, M., Palacios, J., & Román, M. (2020). Executive function and early adversity in internationally adopted children. *Children and Youth Services Review, 108*, 104587. https://doi.org/10.1016/j.childyouth.2019.104587.

Peñarrubia, M., Román, M., & Palacios, J. (2022). Attachment representations and early adversity in internationally adopted children from Russian federation using the friends and family interview. *The Journal of Early Adolescence*, Online First. https://doi.org/10.1177/0272431622 1116050.

Penner, J. (2023). Postadoption service provision: A scoping review, *Adoption Quarterly*, Online publication February 2023. https://doi.org/10.1080/10926755.2023.2176957.

Perry, N. B. & Donzella, B. (2023). Emotion regulation as a predictor of patterns of change in behavior problems in previously institutionalized youth. *Development and Psychopathology*, 1–17. Advance online publication. https://doi.org/10.1017/S0954579423000421.

Pinderhughes, E. & Brodzinsky, D. (2019). Parenting in adoptive families. In M. H. Bornstein (Ed.), *Handbook of Parenting* (3rd ed.,Vol. 1, pp. 322–367). Routledge.

Pinderhughes, E. E., Zhang, X., & Agerbak, S. (2015). "American" or "Multiethnic"? Family ethnic identity among transracial adoptive families, ethnic, racial, socialization, and children' self-perceptions. *New Directions for Child and Adolescent Development, 2015*(150), 5–18. https://doi.org/10.1002/cad.20118.

Plomin, R., Gidziela, A., Malanchini, M., & Von Stumm, S. (2022). Gene–environment interaction using polygenic scores: Do polygenic scores for psychopathology moderate predictions from environmental risk to behavior problems? *Development and Psychopathology, 34*(5), 1816–1826. https://doi.org/10.1017/S0954579422000931.

Popova, S., Charness, M. E., Burd, L. et al. (2023). Fetal alcohol spectrum disorders. *Nature Review Diseases Primers*, *9*, 11. https://doi.org/10.1038/s41572-023-00420-x.

Priel, B., Melamed-Haas, S., Besser, A., & Kantor, B. (2000). Adjustment of adopted children: The role of maternal self-reflectiveness. *Family Relations*, *49*(4), 389–396. https://doi.org/10.1111/j.1741-3729.2000.00389.x.

Raby, K. L. & Dozier, M. (2019). Attachment across the lifespan: Insights from adoptive families. *Current Opinion in Psychology*, *25*, 81–85. https://doi.org/10.1016/j.copsyc.2018.03.011.

Reiss, D., Ganiban, J. M., Leve, L. D. et al. (2023). Parenting in the context of the child: Genetics and social processes. *Monograph of the Society for Research in Child Development*, *87*(1–3). Serial No. 344.

Reuter, M. A. & Koerner, A. F. (2008). The effect of family communication patterns on adopted adolescent adjustment. *Journal of Marriage and Family*, *70*(3), 715–727. https://doi.org/10.1111/j.1741-3737.2008.00516.x.

Riley, D. & Singer, E. (2020). Training for adoption competency curriculum. In G. M. Wrobel, E. Helder, & E. Marr (Eds.), *The Routledge Handbook of Adoption* (pp. 449–463). Routledge.

Rizzo Weller, M. (2022). "I want the piece of paper that is my history, and why the hell can't I have it?": Original birth certificate and adoptive identity. *Journal of Family Communication*, *22*(3), 271–287. https://doi.org/10.1080/15267431.2022.2097234.

Román, M., Palacios, J., & Minnis, H. (2022). Changes in attachment disorder symptoms in children internationally adopted and in residential care. *Child Abuse & Neglect*, *130*(Pt 2), 105308. https://doi.org/10.1016/j.chiabu.2021.105308.

Román. M., Palacios, J., Moreno, C., & López, A. (2012). Attachment representations in internationally adopted children. *Attachment & Human Development*, *14*(6), 585–600.

Rosnati, R. & Ferrari, L. (2014). Parental cultural socialization and perception of discrimination as antecedents for transracial adoptees' ethnic identity. *Procedia – Social & Behavioral Sciences*, *140*, 103–108. https://doi.org/10.1016/j.sbspro.2014.04.393.

Rushton, A. & Dance, C. (2006). The adoption of children from public care: A prospective study of outcomes in adolescence. *Journal of the American Academy of Child and Adolescent Psychiatry*, *45*(7), 877–883.

Rushton, A., Dance, C., & Quinton, D. (2000). Findings from a UK based study of late permanent placements. *Adoption Quarterly*, *3*(3), 51–71. https://doi.org/10.1300/J145v03n03_03.

Rushton, A. & Monck, E. (2009). *Enhancing Adoptive Parenting: A Test of Effectiveness*. British Association for Adoption and Fostering.

Rutter, M. (2006). The promotion of resilience in the face of adversity. In A. Clarke-Stewart & J. Dunn (Eds.),*Families Count: Effects on Child and Adolescent Development* (pp. 26–52). Cambridge University Press. https:// doi.org/10.1017/CBO9780511616259.003.

Rutter, M., Sonuga-Barke, E. J., & Castle, J. I. (2010). Investigating the impact of early institutional deprivation on development: Background and research strategy of the English and Romanian Adoptees (ERA) study. *Monographs of the Society for Research in Child Development, 75*(1), 1–20. https://doi.org/ 10.1111/j.1540-5834.2010.00548.x.

Santos-Nunes, M., Narciso, L., Vieira-Santos, S., & Roberto, M. S. (2018). Adoptive parents' evaluation of expectations and children's behavior problems: The mediational role of parenting stress and parental satisfaction. *Children and Youth Services Review, 88*, 11–17. https://doi.org/10.1016/j .childyouth.2018.02.044.

Schoenmaker, C., Juffer, F., van IJzendoorn, M. H. et al. (2015). Cognitive and health-related outcomes after exposure to early malnutrition: The Leiden longitudinal study of international adoptees. *Children and Youth Services Review, 48*,80–86. https://doi.org/10.1016/j.childyouth.2014.12.010.

Schoemaker, N. K., Wentholt, W. G. M. et al. (2020). A meta-analytic review of parenting interventions in foster care and adoption. *Development and Psychopathology, 32*(3), 1149–1172. https://doi.org/10.1017/S095457941 9000798.

Scott, K. A., Roberts, J. A., & Glennen, S. (2011). How well do children who are internationally adopted acquire language? A meta-analysis. *Journal of Speech, Language, and Hearing Research, 54*(4), 1153–1169. https://doi .org/10.1044/1092-4388(2010/10-0075.

Séguin-Baril, S. & Saint-Jacques, M. C. (2023). A scoping review and a critical analysis of the international adoption research field in the social sciences. *Adoption Quarterly, 26*(2), 138–185. https://doi.org/10.1080/10926755 .2022.2156009.

Sharma, A. R., McGue, M. K., & Benson, P. L. (1996). The emotional and behavioral adjustment of United States adopted adolescents: Part 1. An overview. *Children and Youth Services Review, 18*(1–2), 83–100. https:// doi.org/10.1016/0190-7409(95)00055-0.

Shewark, E. A., Ramos, A. M., Liu, C. et al. (2021). The role of child negative emotionality in parenting and child adjustment: Gene-environment interplay. *Journal of Child Psychology and Psychiatry, 62*(12), 1453–1461. https://doi .org/10.1111/jcpp.13420.

Smith, S. & Howard, J. (1999). *Promoting Successful Adoptions: Practice with Troubled Families*. Sage.

Sonuga-Barke, E. J. S., Kennedy, M., Kumsta, R. et al. (2017). Child-to-adult neurodevelopmental and mental health trajectories after early life deprivation: The young adult follow-up of the longitudinal English and Romanian Adoptees study. *Lancet, 389*(10078), 1539–1548. https://doi.org/10.1016/S0140-6736(17)30045-4.

Sorosky, A., Baran, A., & Pannor, R. (1975). Identity conflicts in adoptees. *American Journal of Orthopsychiatry, 45*(1), 18–27. https://doi/10.1111/j.1939-0025.1975.tb01162.x.

Sue, D. W. (Ed.). (2010). *Microaggressions and Marginality: Manifestation, Dynamics, and Impact*. Wiley.

Sue, D. W., Bucceri, J., Lin, A. I., Nadal, K. L., & Torino, G. C. (2007). Racial microaggressions and the Asian American experience. *Cultural Diversity and Ethnic Minority Psychology, 13*(1), 72–81. https://psycnet.apa.org/doi/10.1037/1948-1985.S.1.88.

Tang, E., Bleys, D., & Vliegen, N. (2018). Making sense of adopted children's internal reality using narrative story stem techniques: A mixed-methods synthesis. *Frontiers in Psychology, 9*, 1189. https://doi.org/10.3389/fpsyg.2018.01189.

Tasker, F. & Lavender-Stott, E. S. (2020). LGBTQ parenting post-heterosexual relationship dissolution. In A. E. Goldberg & K. R. Allen (Eds.), *LGBTQ Parent Families: Innovations in Research and Implications for Practice* (pp. 3–24) (2nd ed.). Springer.

Tieman, W., van der Ende, J., & Verhulst, F. C. (2008). Young adult international adoptees' search for birth parents. *Journal of Family Psychology, 22* (5), 678–687. https://doi.org/10.1037/a0013172.

Tienari, P., Wynne, L. C., Sorri, A. et al. (2004). Genotype-environment interaction in schizophrenia-spectrum disorder: Long-term follow-up study of Finnish adoptees. *British Journal of Psychiatry, 184*, 216–222. https://doi.org/10.1192/bjp.184.3.216.

van der Voort, A., Linting, M., Juffer, F. et al. (2014). The development of adolescents' internalizing behavior: Longitudinal effects of maternal sensitivity and child inhibition. *Journal of Youth and Adolescence, 43*, 528–540. https://doi.org/10.1007/s10964-013-9976-7.

Van IJzendoorn, M. H., Schuengel, C., Wang, Q., & Bakermans-Kranenburg, M.J. (2023). Improving parenting, child attachment, and externalizing behaviors: Meta-analysis of the first 25 randomized controlled trials on the effects of video-feedback Intervention to promote positive parenting and sensitive discipline. *Development and Psychopathology, 35*(1), 241–256, https://doi.org/10.1017/S0954579421001462.

van IJzendoorn, M. H., Bakermans-Kranenburg, M. J., Coughlan, B., & Reijman, S. (2019). Umbrella synthesis of meta-analyses on child maltreatment antecedents and interventions: Differential susceptibility perspective on risk and resilience. *Journal of Child Psychology and Psychiatry, 61*(3), 272–290. https://doi.org/10.1111/jcpp.13147.

Van IJzendoorn, M. H., Bakermans-Kranenburg, M. J., & Juffer, F. (2007). Plasticity of growth in height, weight, and head circumference: Meta-analytic evidence of massive catch-up after international adoption. *Journal of Developmental Behavioral Pediatrics, 2007, 28*(4), 334–343. https://doi.org/10.1097/DBP.0b013e31811320aa.

van IJzendoorn, M. H. & Juffer, F. (2006). Adoption as intervention. Meta-analytic evidence of massive catch-up and plasticity in physical, socio-emotional, and cognitive development. *Journal of Child Psychology and Psychiatry, 47*, 1228–1245. https://doi.org/10.1111/j.1469-7610.2006.01675.x.

van IJzendoorn, M. H., Juffer, F., & Klein Poelhuis, C. W. (2005). Adoption and cognitive development: A meta-analytic comparison of adopted and non-adopted children's IQ and school performance. *Psychological Bulletin, 131*(2), 301–316. https://doi.org/10.1037/0033-2909.131.2.301.

Viana, A. G. & Welsh, J. A. (2010). Correlates and predictors of parenting stress among internationally adopting mothers: A longitudinal investigation. *International Journal of Behavioral Development, 34*(4), 363–373. https://doi.org/10.1177/0165025409339403.

Von Korff, L. & Grotevant, H. D. (2011). Contact in adoption and adoptive identity formation: The mediating role of family conversation. *Journal of . Family Psychology, 25*(3), 393–401. https://doi/10.1037/a0023388.

Von Korff, L., Grotevant, H. D., & McRoy, R. G. (2006). Openness in adoption arrangements and psychological adjustment in adolescent adoptees. *Journal of Family Psychology, 20*(3), 393–401. https://psycnet.apa.org/doi/10.1037/0893-3200.20.3.531.

von Stumm, S. & d'Apice, K. (2022). From genome-wide to environment-wide: Capturing the environome. *Perspectives on Psychological Science, 17*(1), 30–40. https://doi.org/10.1177/1745691620979803.

Wade, M., Fox, N. A., Zeanah, C. H., & Nelson, C. A. (2019). Long-term effects of institutional rearing, foster care, and brain activity on memory and executive functioning. *Proceedings of the National Academy of Sciences, 16*(5), 1808–1813. https://doi:10.1073/pnas.1809145116.

Wade, M., Parson, J., Humphreys, K. A., et al. (2022). The bucharest early intervention project: Adolescent mental health and adaptation following early deprivation. *Child Development Perspectives*, *16*(3), 157–164. doi: https://doi.org10.1111/cdep.12462.

Wade, M., Zeanah, C. H., Fox, N. A., & Nelson, C. A. (2020). Global deficits in executive functioning are transdiagnostic mediators between severe childhood neglect and psychopathology in adolescence. *Psychological Medicine*, *50*(10), 1687–1694. https://doi.org/10.1017/S0033291719001764.

Waid, J. & Alewine, E. (2018). An exploration of family challenges and service needs during the postadoption period. *Children and Youth Services Review*, *91*, 213–220. https://psycnet.apa.org/doi/10.1016/jchildyouth.2018.06.017.

Ward, H., Moggach, L., Tregeagle, S., & Trivedi, H. (2022). *Outcomes of Open Adoption from Care: An Australian Contribution to an International Debate*. Springer Nature.

Warren S. B. (1992). Lower threshold for referral for psychiatric treatment for adopted adolescents. *Journal of the American Academy of Child and Adolescent Psychiatry*, *31*(3), 512–517. https://doi.org/10.1097/00004583-199205000-00019.

Waterman, J., Langley, A. K., Miranda, J., & Riley, D. (2018). *Adoption-Specific Therapy: A Guide to Helping Adopted Children and their Families Thrive*. American Psychological Association.

Wind, L. H., Brooks, D., & Barth, R. P. (2007). Influences of risk history and adoption preparation on postadoption services use in U.S. adoptions. *Family Relations*, *56*(4), 378–389. https://doi.org/10.1111/j.1741-3729.2007.00467.x.

Wretham, A. E. & Woolgar, M. (2017). Do children adopted from British foster care show difficulties in executive functioning and social communication? *Adoption & Fostering*, *41*(4), 331–345. https://doi.org/10.1177/0308575917730295.

Wrobel, G. M. & Dillon, K. (2009). Adopted adolescents: Who and what are they curious about? In G. M. Wrobel & E. Neil (Eds.), *International Advances in Adoption Research and Practice* (pp. 217–244). Wiley.

Wrobel, G. M. & Grotevant, H. D. (2019). Minding the (information) gap: What do emerging adult adoptees want to know about their birth parents? *Adoption Quarterly*, *22*(1), 29–52. https://doi.org/10.1080/10926755.2018.1488332.

Wrobel, G. M., Kohler, J. K., Grotevant, H. D., & McRoy, R. G. (2003). The family adoption communication (FAC) model. *Adoption Quarterly*, *7*(2), 53–84. https://doi.org/10.1300/J145v07n02_04.

Zeegers, M. A. J., Colonnes, C., Noom, M. J., Polderman, N., & Stams, G-J. J. M. (2020). Remediating child attachment insecurity: Evaluating the basic trust intervention in adoptive families. *Research on Social Work Practice*, *30*(7), 736–749. https://psycnet.apa.org/doi/10.1177/1049731519863106.

Zeegers, M. A. J., de Vente, W., Nikolic, M. et al. (2018). Mothers' and fathers' mind-mindedness influence physiological emotion regulation of infants across the first year. *Developmental Science, 21*(6), e12689. https://doi.org/10.1111/desc.12689.

Zhang, E., Zhang, X., & Pinderhughes, E. E. (2019). "Your skin's not as good as us": Microaggressions among transracially adopted children from China. *Adoption Quarterly, 22*(4), 284–306. https://doi.org/10.1080/10926755.2019.1675837.

Zima, B. T., Bussing, R., Yang, X., & Belin, T. R. (2000). Help-seeking steps and service use for children in foster care. *Journal of Behavioral Health Services & Research, 27*(3), 271–285. https://psycnet.apa.org/doi/10.1007/BF02291739.

Zwaanswijk, M., Verhaak, P. F. M., van der Ende, J., Bensing, J. M., & Verhulst, F. C. (2006). Change in children's emotional and behavioral problems over a one-year period: Associations with parental problem recognition and service use. *European Child & Adolescent Psychiatry, 13*(3), 127–131. https://psycnet.apa.org/doi/10.1007/s00787-005-0513-4.

In memory of Irv Sigel, who stimulated our passion for the study of children and their families long before we met. Years later he served as a bridge to the beginning of our long-lasting collaboration.

Cambridge Elements ≡

Child Development

Marc H. Bornstein

National Institute of Child Health and Human Development, Bethesda
Institute for Fiscal Studies, London
UNICEF, New York City

Marc H. Bornstein is an Affiliate of the *Eunice Kennedy Shriver* National Institute of Child Health and Human Development, an International Research Fellow at the Institute for Fiscal Studies (London), and UNICEF Senior Advisor for Research for ECD Parenting Programmes. Bornstein is President Emeritus of the Society for Research in Child Development, Editor Emeritus of *Child Development*, and founding Editor of *Parenting: Science and Practice.*

About the Series

Child development is a lively and engaging, yet serious and real-world subject of scientific study that encompasses myriad theories, methods, substantive areas, and applied concerns. Cambridge Elements in Child Development addresses many contemporary topics in child development with unique, comprehensive, and state-of-the-art treatments of principal issues, primary currents of thinking, original perspectives, and empirical contributions to understanding early human development.

Cambridge Elements ≡

Child Development

Elements in the Series

A full series listing is available at: www.cambridge.org/EICD

Printed in the United States
by Baker & Taylor Publisher Services